best
hikes
with

dogs

CENTRAL CALIFORNIA

D1132504

best
hikes
with
dogs

CENTRAL CALIFORNIA

**Linda Mullally &
David Mullally**

THE MOUNTAINEERS BOOKS

Dedication

To Lobo and Shiloh, and all the dogs waiting over Rainbow Bridge.

THE MOUNTAINEERS BOOKS
is the nonprofit publishing arm of The Mountaineers Club, an organization founded in 1906 and dedicated to the exploration, preservation, and enjoyment of outdoor and wilderness areas.

1001 SW Klickitat Way, Suite 201, Seattle, WA 98134

© 2008 by Linda Mullally and David Mullally

All rights reserved

First edition, 2008

No part of this book may be reproduced in any form, or by any electronic, mechanical, or other means, without permission in writing from the publisher.

Manufactured in the United States of America

Acquiring Editor: Dana Youlin
Project Editor: Janet Kimball
Copy Editor: Joeth Zucco
Cover and Book Design: The Mountaineers Books
Layout: Jennifer Shontz, Red Shoe Design
Cartographer: Jennifer Shontz, Red Shoe Design
Photographer: David Mullally
Author photograph: Dan McCormick

Cover photograph: *Moses is always ready for a good hike.*
Frontispiece: *A long, cold drink along the Saddlebag Lake Trail*
Maps shown in this book were produced using National Geographic's TOPO! software. For more information, go to *www.nationalgeographic.com/topo.*

Library of Congress Cataloging-in-Publication Data
Mullally, Linda B.
    Best hikes with dogs : central California / Linda Mullally and David Mullally.
— 1st ed.
        p.   cm.
    Includes index.
    ISBN 978-1-59485-049-3 (ppb)
    1. Hiking with dogs—California—Guidebooks. 2.
Trails—California—Guidebooks. 3. California—Guidebooks. I. Mullally, David.
II. Title.
SF427.455.M84 2008
796.5109794—dc22

                                                                  2007043507

 Printed on recycled paper

CONTENTS

HIKE SUMMARY TABLE

KEY:

Fido fitness scale: F=fit X=extremely fit L=limited fitness

Off leash: Y=yes P=partial

Cool and wet: C=creek L=lake P=pond O=ocean R=river

Hike	Up to 5 miles	Over 5 miles	Above 6000 feet	Fido fitness scale	Off leash	Cool and wet	Shade	Campground	Backpacking
1. Pipeline Road		•		FX			•	•	
2. Skyline Nature Trail to Jacks Peak	•			FXL			•		
3. Huckleberry Hill Loop	•			FX	Y		•	•	
4. Monterey Bay Coastal Recreational Trail to Asilomar State Beach		•		FXL	P	O			
5. Spanish Bay to Bird Rock	•			FXL	P	O			
6. Carmel Beach	•			FXL	P	O			
7. Carmel Meadows	•			FXL		O			
8. Mission Trail Loop	•			FXL	Y		•		
9. El Toro Creek–Skyline Road Loop		•		FXL	Y				
10. Ollason Trail to Simas Peak		•		FXL	P		•		
11. Snivleys Ridge		•		FXL	Y	PRC	•		
12. Garzas Canyon to Redwood Canyon	•			FX	Y	C	•		
13. Los Padres Dam to Carmel River Campsite		•		FXL	Y	R	•		•
14. Pfeiffer Beach	•			FXL	P	O		•	
15. East Cuesta Ridge		•		FX	Y				
16. Merced River Trail	•			FXL	Y	R		•	
17. Lewis Creek National Scenic Trail		•		FXL	Y	C	•		
18. Dinkey Lakes		•	•	FX	Y	L	•	•	•
19. Rancheria Falls	•		•	FXL	Y			•	
20. Boole Tree Loop	•		•	FXL	Y		•	•	
21. Chicago Stump Trail	•		•	FXL	Y		•	•	
22. Weaver Lake		•	•	FX	Y	L	•	•	
23. Chiquito Pass		•	•	FX	Y	L	•	•	
24. Nunatak Nature Trail	•		•	FXL	Y	P	•	•	
25. Glacier Canyon	•		•	FXL	Y	CL	•	•	
26. Gardisky Lake	•		•	FX	Y	L	•	•	
27. Saddlebag Lake	•		•	FXL	Y	L		•	

Hike	Up to 5 miles	Over 5 miles	Above 6000 feet	Fido fitness scale	Off leash	Cool and wet	Shade	Campground	Backpacking
28. Fern Lake	•		•	FX	Y	L	•	•	
29. Yost Lake	•		•	FX	Y	L	•	•	
30. Sherwin Lakes	•		•	FX	Y	L	•	•	
31. Valentine Lake		•	•	FX	Y	L	•	•	
32. Laurel Lakes		•	•	X	Y	LC		•	•
33. Rainbow Falls		•	•	FX	P	R		•	
34. Minaret Falls	•		•	FXL	P	R	•	•	
35. Panorama Dome	•		•	FXL	Y			•	
36. Horseshoe Lake	•		•	FXL	Y	L	•	•	
37. McLeod Lake	•		•	FXL	Y	L	•	•	
38. Emerald Lake	•		•	FXL	Y	L	•	•	
39. Crystal Lake	•		•	FX	Y	L	•	•	
40. Convict Lake Loop	•		•	FXL	Y	L	•	•	
41. McGee Creek		•	•	FX	Y	C		•	
42. Gem Lakes		•	•	FX	Y	L		•	•
43. Chocolate Lakes Loop		•	•	FX	Y	L	•	•	•
44. Grass Lake	•		•	FXL	Y	L	•	•	
45. Lake Sabrina	•		•	FX	Y	L		•	
46. First Falls and Second Falls	•		•	FX	Y	C		•	
47. Bristlecone Pine Forest Discovery Trail	•		•	FXL				•	
48. Kearsarge Pass		•	•	FX	Y	LC		•	•
49. Lone Pine Lake		•	•	FX	Y	L	•	•	
50. Fossil Falls	•			FXL	Y			•	
51. Bald Mountain	•		•	FXL	Y		•		
52. Dome Rock	•		•	FXL	Y			•	
53. Trail of 100 Giants	•		•	FXL	Y		•	•	
54. North Fork Kern River Trail	•			FXL	Y	R		•	
55. Sunday Peak	•		•	FX	Y		•	•	

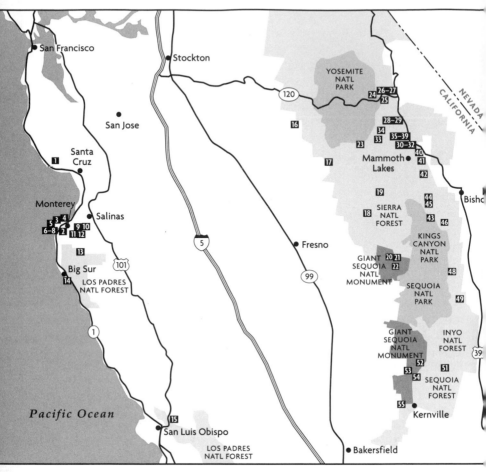

LEGEND

══════════	Interstate Highway
──────────	Paved Road
══════════	Dirt Road
■■■■■■■■■■	Featured Trail
··········	Connecting Trail
─ · ─ · ─ ·	Wilderness Boundary
	River/Creek/Falls
	Lake
90	Interstate
87	U.S. Highway
530	State Route
14S11	Forest Road

T	Trailhead
P	Parking
⚠	Campground
▲	Peak
■	Building
☀	Lighthouse
) (	Pass
] [	Bridge
•—•	Gate
★	Scenic View
⊼	Picnic Table

ACKNOWLEDGMENTS

I could not have committed to this project without my husband, David, as a co-author. Our joint passion for the outdoors has made for happy trails. His appetite for new challenges and his legendary optimism helped me overcome my techno-phobia and turned frustration into laughter when the GPS developed a mind of its own.

Thank you to our fellow dog lovers and friends: Shellie Reade and Harold Matzner, Priscilla and John Walton, and Liz and Scott Kantor for trusting us with the care and education of their beloved dogs, Alex, Murphy, and Moses. We couldn't have asked for more responsive hiking companions whose enthusiasm and affection enriched every mile on the trails.

We also want to thank our many other outdoors-loving friends who hike with their photogenic pooches including Christie and Tim Doyle with Saorla, one of the lucky Katrina rescues; Molly and Mikko Attell with their perky pack of seniors, Sequoia, Chitsa, and Dakota; Shellie and Robert Reade with little Stanley; and Harold Matzner with sweet Spencer.

Dr. George Bishop, our family veterinarian, deserves our gratitude for years of consistently sound advice and his contribution to this book.

We are grateful for Park Ranger Robert Chapin at Garland Ranch Regional Park who always greets hikers and their dogs with friendliness, never too busy to answer questions, and believes the more you educate the less you have to penalize.

Thank you to Ranger Kitty Van Stelle and Ranger Tim Bue at the Mammoth Lakes Visitor Center and United States Forest Service Ranger Station for their eagerness to share their knowledge. We extend an equal note of appreciation to all the dog-loving rangers and park administrators at the city, county, state, and federal levels who were so supportive of this book and patiently guided me through the bureaucratic maze on my quest for accurate information.

PREFACE

I t was the life-altering arrival of two free-spirited and challenging husky-coyote hybrids that led my husband and me on a sixteen-year path of adventure, daily hikes, backpacking journeys, and explorations from coast to coast in the United States and Canada. Although we knew little of what we were getting into when we naively welcomed Lobo and Shiloh into our home and committed to putting their safety, happiness, and well-being first, we are forever grateful for the gift of entering their world and reconnecting more intimately with nature.

This is my second hiking book. Lobo and Shiloh inspired the first, and although they were not here to share the adventures of this book, I feel that the sixteen years of life on the trails was the prelude to writing this guide and implementing many lessons learned from our wild companions. The biggest challenge in writing this book became its biggest reward. Slowing my pace on the trail allowed me to absorb beauty previously gone unnoticed. I was reminded of how Lobo and Shiloh had taught me to see, listen, and feel beyond looking, hearing, and touching in order to appreciate nature's more subtle gifts.

Sitting on a boulder at Gardisky Lake, I had the first hint of mixed feelings about sharing that hike and other similar pristine places with dog owners. Gardisky Lake, a dog-friendly and stellar setting on the threshold of Yosemite National Park, is undeniably worthy of adorning the crown of our national park system. Were it not for the fluke of boundaries, dogs would be banned at Gardisky Lake. It was there that I realized how jewels like Gardisky Lake are precious opportunities for dog owners to demonstrate their greatest sense of responsibility to a fragile environment, where plant and animal life can go from thriving to struggling at a season's notice. Good stewardship, I believe, is the first step in extending a welcome to our four-legged friends on national park trails as enjoyed by our Canadian cousins and their dogs, in their own equally precious nature sanctuaries.

If there is such a thing as Godliness, then I believe that nature in its infinite facets and proportions is its only true portal, and what better guides and companions than our dogs on this sublime journey.

PART 1

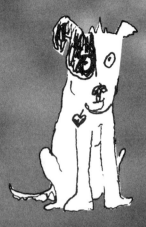

Before You Step on the Trail

Good Dogs Have Good Owners

You've heard the phrase, "there are no bad dogs, just bad owners." Giving humans the benefit of the doubt, with the exception of a few criminally cruel individuals, most bad dog behavior is created or reinforced by well-intentioned, albeit poorly trained and misinformed, dog owners.

The building blocks to being a good dog owner with a good dog are the right motivation and a compatible match to your personality and lifestyle. Good dog owners begin with room in their hearts, time in their life, and extra money in their budget to care for a devoted companion as a cherished family member.

When dog fever strikes, consider these "reality checks" for the best fit:

1. **Puppy love has hidden costs.** Sleep deprivation, messy housebreaking routines, frustrating chewing habits, weeks of demanding feeding, and attention schedules. If you can't afford to meet the needs of raising a puppy, there are many wonderful, housebroken adult dogs waiting to be adopted through shelters and breed rescue clubs.

2. **All dogs grow up to become old dogs.** Be prepared for the fact that the senior years can be as high maintenance as puppyhood.

3. **Dogs cost money.** The exciting shopping spree for the new leash and collar (depending on the breed, puppies will outgrow at least two collars before they're full grown), healthy chow formula, dog bed, and toy to welcome pooch into your life is just the beginning. Veterinary care priorities include spaying or neutering and vaccinations. A veterinary consult and a cheap prescription might get you off easy with some unexpected mishaps, but in some cases treatment may be more costly. Diagnostic tests and surgery are sure to amp your bill.

4. **Living quarters matter.** At 3:00 AM when pooch has to go out, dog ownership will look different to the person on the fifteenth floor of the condominium than to the person in the house with the fenced backyard.

5. **Lifestyle choices.** Whether a dog is content to sit in your lap between walks from your downtown studio apartment, or needs to patrol your ten-acre homestead from sunrise to sunset in order to thrive (and some do), all need companionship from humans or from other pets (in your absence) to satisfy their pack instinct.

6. **Doggie disposition.** Territorial and high-strung dogs deserve the same unconditional love as affable and mellow dogs. But

these personality traits will impact your lifestyle and your dog's suitability for the trail.

7. **Exercise needs.** Is pooch a keener or a lounger? Picking a dog that is on the same "physical activity" page will make life more enjoyable for both of you.

8. **Physical characteristics and grooming.** Maintenance must be compatible with the climate you live in and play in. A husky's frost-loving undercoat, a Chihuahua's fun-in-the-sun short hair, and a Portuguese water dog's Velcro-like curls are better suited to some trails than others.

9. **Breed-specific genetic vulnerabilities.** Is there a predisposition to hip and joint problems, skin conditions, respiratory difficulties, or other health conditions that may impact your activities together as well as your wallet? If you go for the puppy, ask your veterinarian about pet health insurance.

10. **Training is essential and bad habits die hard.** Dog owners have to invest time and patience into training their dog. In class environments, owners are as much the pupil as their dog.

Breed books and clubs, animal shelters, and your veterinarian are all good resources in guiding you on your search of a healthy, compatible companion.

Dog Myths and Misunderstandings

Big dogs rule. Bigger dogs are not necessarily hardier or better hikers. Some small breeds, Jack Russell terriers, for example, have more stamina on the trail than some of their larger cousins. Bernese mountain dogs' slow-growing bones prohibit strenuous exercise and hills for the first couple of years.

Spaying and neutering makes dogs fat and lazy. Too much food, the wrong foods, and a lack of exercise makes dogs fat. With regards to disposition, neutering decreases a male dog's desire to roam the neighborhood and tones down his "macho" gene when in the company of other male dogs; spaying makes female dogs less boy crazy and less competitive with other females. Your dog's IQ and perky personality will be intact. Healthwise, it reduces the risks of prostate and mammary gland cancers, as well as helps curb overpopulation and euthanasia.

Babysitters and home alarms. Dogs should be family pets, not tools or conveniences. Getting a dog as a playmate in order to teach children responsibility is inappropriate and unfair to the dog. Staking

Checkerspot butterfly

a dog out in the yard with a doghouse and a bowl of water, to bark and intimidate would-be trespassers is abusive. Dogs deserve and need physical and mental stimulation, affection, outdoor exercise, good training, and social interaction with other canines and their human pack (family), in addition to a healthy diet and veterinary care, in order to be thriving, well-adjusted, and happy pets.

Smart dogs always find their way home. It's a comforting thought, but an identification tag with contact information attached to a collar is a much more reliable way to be reunited with your dog if he gets lost. Be aware that rain and snow can interfere with a dog's scent, so keep closer track of your dog if hiking under such conditions, especially in new territory. When in doubt, snap on the leash.

Dogs damage trails. Out-of-control dogs off leash create an unacceptable nuisance and risk on the trail and usually belong to poorly trained humans. These same poorly trained people (on foot, on bike, or on horseback) are usually the ones who cut off trail switchbacks, discard candy wrappers on the ground, leave trash in the campsite, and have poorly trained children. The latter are far more likely to damage trails than dogs. Stock animals do their share of trail damage as well.

Canine Ten Essentials Plus

1. **Obedience training and trail manners.** Before you set foot on a trail, make sure your dog is trained and can be trusted to behave when faced with other hikers, other dogs, wildlife, and an assortment of strange scents and sights in the backcountry. It's just a matter of training *you* to train your dog into the best-mannered hiker he can be. Puppy class gives you a head start on the basic drills that will translate into good trail manners. If you have an adult dog, your veterinarian, breed club, local shelter, or pet supply store can assist you in locating a good trainer or group class.

    All dogs should be responsive to at least three basic commands before setting paw on the trail: *no, sit,* and *stay. Come,* the most coveted and lofty training goal, requires long-term, consistent positive reinforcement. Until you are 100 percent confident of your dog's responsiveness on recall off leash, a leash is the only way to guarantee his safety and to protect habitat and wildlife from his zealous antics.

2. **Doggy backpack.** Adult dogs of thirty pounds or more can be gradually trained to carry their own gear. The total weight (including packs) should be evenly distributed and not exceed more than a quarter to a third (large breeds) of your dog's weight. Less is better. Dogs are companions, not beasts of burden. Placing a towel on your dog's back when he's walking around the house is a good way to get him use to the feel of weight on his back before stepping it up to the empty pack.

3. **Basic first-aid kit.** Your dog's first-aid kit can be combined with yours as several items serve both (details listed below).

4. **Dog food and trail treats.** Ideally adult dogs should be fed twice daily (pups more often). On a strenuous hike, it's a good idea to feed half of the breakfast portion before starting out and the other half at lunch break. Pack an extra portion for the afternoon since your dog will be burning more calories than normal. Serving several smaller portions throughout the day will be easier on his digestive system and help prevent bloat in the case of more vulnerable, larger, deep-chested dogs. Trail treats serve the same purpose for your dog as they do for you—quick energy boosters and a pick-me-up during a strenuous day of hiking. Protein dog treats are great energy supplements along the trail.

If you're camping out, make sure to pack enough food for every meal on the trail and extra portions in the event you end up spending an extra night out. Rice and pasta are lightweight, easy to cook, and a tasty addition to his kibbles.

5. **Water and bowl.** Don't count on finding water along the trail; pack enough extra water to meet your dog's drinking needs. Even with a purifier for streams and lakes, some dogs won't drink water that has been treated. Consider the temperatures (hotter, drier, and higher means more dehydration). You should have at least eight ounces of water per dog for every one hour or 2 miles of trail. Remember HEAD—Heat, Exertion, Altitude, and Dehydration—the four most common and preventable hiking hazards for you and pooch. Recyclable plastic or heavy paper bowls or resealable plastic freezer bags (one-gallon type) make good lightweight improvisations if you don't have a collapsible dog bowl in your pack.

6. **Leash and collar or harness.** Even if your dog is absolutely trained to voice command and heels without a leash, sometimes leashes are required by law, as a common courtesy, or as a safety tool on precarious stretches of trail or stream crossings. Always carry one. A loose chain choker collar can lead to injury or death and is an absolute no-no when your dog is off leash. Even as a training tool, head halters are preferred and considered more humane by an increasing number of trainers.

Mallard ducks at Fern Lake

A properly fitted harness is comfortable and much safer on the trail. If your dog lost his footing on a narrow trail or crossing, you would want his leash attached to his back, not to his neck.

7. **Insect repellent.** Ticks and fleas are present in many of the areas you will hike in this book. Since any tick or flea product (the monthly liquid applications between the shoulder blades or repellent collars) already exposes your dog to chemicals, consider a natural alternative to DEET-based repellents containing eucalyptus or lavender. If you must use a DEET-based repellent, be aware that some animals—and some people—have strong negative reactions to it. Before leaving home, dab a little DEET-based repellent on a patch of your dog's fur to see if he reacts. Look for signs of drowsiness, lethargy, and nausea. Apply repellent to places the dog can't lick—the back of the neck and around the ears (staying well clear of the outer and inner ears) are the most logical places mosquitoes will be looking for exposed skin to bite.

8. **ID tags and picture identification.** Your dog should always wear an ID tag. Micro-chipping—a process where a vet injects a tiny encoded microchip under the skin between the dog's shoulders—is very popular and effective for reuniting dogs and owners between the hours of 9:00 AM and 5:00 PM, Monday through Friday, when someone is available to scan the animal. But at odd hours, in odd places, I'd place my bet on a good old-fashioned ID tag with your dog's name and your telephone number (both home and cell phone numbers). If you have a base camp for a few nights in a campground or at a cabin, consider a temporary tag with the campground name or the cabin resort name and number.

The picture identification should go in your pack. If your dog gets lost, you can use the photo to make flyers to post in the surrounding communities.

9. **Dog booties.** These can be used to protect the dog's paws from rough ground or harsh vegetation. You should have your dog get used to wearing the booties in the house in case he ever needs to wear them on the trail. To avoid damage to the pads, your dog's paws should be conditioned over a period of time to longer hikes over varied terrain, so the surface of the pads gradually thickens and toughens. Watch his gait for signs of tenderness before the damage occurs. I've had to carry a ten-pound dog for the last 2

miles out of the backcountry. You wouldn't want to try that with a Labrador. Booties are also great at keeping bandages secure if the dog injures its pads.

10. **Compact roll of biodegradable plastic bags and trowel.** You'll need bags to clean up after your dog on popular trails. Look for dispensers at some of the trailheads in county- and city-administered parklands. Check your local pet supply store for the latest eco-friendly innovations in disposable doggie-doo bags. When conditions warrant, you can use the trowel to take care of dog waste. Dig a small hole four- to six-inches deep in the forest duff, deposit the dog waste, and fill in the hole.

Plus

Doggie fashion. Thin, shorthair dogs unaccustomed to colder weather need an extra layer. Purchase a sweater suitable for foggy, chilly conditions on the coast or sudden, extreme weather in the Sierra.

   Dog brush, towels, and eau de skunk shampoo. Brush your dog back at the car or in camp to remove foxtails, burrs, or ticks. A dog towel in the trunk or in camp comes in handy for a wet or dirty dog at the end of the trail. In the unfortunate event of a too close encounter with Fifi le Pew, keep a bottle of homemade shampoo in the car or in your overnight pack.

Shampoo Recipe
1 quart 3 percent hydrogen peroxide, $1/4$ cup baking soda, 1 tablespoon dishwashing liquid, and juice from two lemons.

A Doggie First-Aid Kit
Having a dog first-aid kit is necessary, even if it has only the bare bones essentials. For a comprehensive canine first-aid kit, carry the following essentials:

Instruments
- Scissors, bandage scissors, toenail clippers
- Tweezers
- Rectal thermometer (a healthy dog shows a temperature of 101°F rectally)

Cleansers and disinfectants

- 3 percent hydrogen peroxide to clean wounds
- Betadine to sterilize
- Prepackaged alcohol swabs (useful on dogs' pads, to cool dogs with heatstroke in dry terrain)
- Canine eyewash (available at large pet supply stores)
- Topical antibiotics, analgesics, and ointments (over the counter)
- Triple antibiotic ointment (Neosporin)
- Topical analgesic spray for bee stings (Benadryl)
- Antihistamine (over the counter; consult your veterinarian on dosage)
- Vaseline
- Stop-bleeding powder

Medications

- Buffered Ascriptin for pain relief (consult your veterinarian on dosage)
- Pepto-Bismol (immediate, short-term remedy for upset stomach)
- Pepcid AC (once daily as preventative and all-day treatment)
- Emetic (a super-saturated salt and water solution that induces vomiting)

Dressings and bandages

- Gauze pads (4-inch square) or gauze roll
- Nonstick pads
- Adhesive tape (1- and 2-inch rolls)
- Duct tape
- Cling wrap

Miscellaneous

- Muzzle (even the sweetest dogs can snap in reaction to pain; put the muzzle on before treating a sore or injured dog)
- Booties (improvise with a sock and duct tape if necessary)
- Prescription medication that your dog is on (consult your veterinarian on any other remedies he would recommend in emergency situations)
- Your veterinarian's telephone number
- National poison hotline telephone number: 888-426-4435

Your Ten Essentials Plus

1. **Navigation** (map, compass, GPS)
2. **Sun protection** (sunglasses, hat, sunscreen, lip balm)

3. **Insulation** (extra clothing). On the trail, wear breathable layers for comfort and insulation, including wicking fabric for the first layer; windproof rain pants and jacket with hood, plastic rain ponchos, or oversize plastic trash bags to keep you and your gear dry; and waterproof hiking boots (carry lightweight water footwear, preferably closed toe with traction, for stream crossings). Warm gloves and hat for the Sierra. In your vehicle or pack, carry a change of socks and footwear and a fresh shirt.
4. **Illumination** (headlamp or flashlight)
5. **First-aid supplies**—(consolidate your first-aid kit with pooch's by adding Band-Aids and Nuskin for blisters)
6. **Fire** (firestarter and waterproof matches or lighter)
7. **Repair kit and tools** (Swiss army knife)
8. **Nutrition** (extra food, energy snacks including protein bars, dried fruit, nuts, dark chocolate)
9. **Hydration** (extra water and water purifier)
10. **Emergency shelter** (plastic tarp or space blanket and rope)

Plus

Cardio Pulmonary Resuscitation. Enroll in a CPR class through your local Red Cross chapter or fire department, and check with your veterinarian or local humane society on pet CPR. These agencies may offer first-aid classes as well.

Hiking poles. Adjustable poles with pointed ends and baskets are great on steep inclines (up and down) and for crossing streams or snowfields.

Tecnu. A liquid soap wash for poison oak.

Backpacking Extras

Clothing. River sandals for camp, extra socks, shirt, long pants

Food and water. Rice, pasta, tuna, and dehydrated meals from outdoor recreation stores are lightweight, nutritious, easy to prepare, and can be added to your dog's kibbles

Cooking. Gas stove with extra gas

Housekeeping. A tie-out line for your pooch and a foam pad or water-resistant blanket for pooch while in camp. Don't put food in the tent to guard it. Use resealable freezer bags for garbage and sealing any odiferous goods from bears' keen noses, and use bear-proof storage canisters for food and scented goods, including soaps and cosmetics. Most developed campsites have bear-proof storage bins. In the backcountry, hang your food and garbage four feet from tree trunks and ten feet off the ground . Pack it in, pack it out.

Shelter. A tent large enough to accommodate you and your dog(s), pad and sleeping bag for you, foam roll-up or water-resistant dog blanket for him.

Home alone. Never leave your dog unattended in camp. It's unsafe and unkind for him and inconsiderate to other campers who may have to suffer the howls and barks of separation anxiety.

Health and Safety and Preventative Care

Practicing a few simple preventative care routines ahead of time will help optimize your dog's health, safety, and mutual enjoyment on the trail. On the trail, there's only one rule that matters: "Your dog's well being comes first." Make your choices and decisions accordingly every time.

Fitness. Be realistic about your dog's limitations (breed, fitness, age) when choosing a hike. Your veterinarian should help you evaluate your dog's general health condition and fitness level based on his age and medical history. Just like human couch potatoes, a sedentary or overweight dog can be conditioned into a fit hiker with proper diet and a gradual exercise regime.

Vaccinations. Follow your veterinarian's recommendations on vaccinations and make sure your dog is current on rabies before hitting the trail. Some park agencies require proof of rabies vaccination at the entrance.

Grooming. Nails should be trimmed for comfort and traction (too long is as bad as too short). High-maintenance coats and long, lustrous ground-sweeping coats are nightmares on the trail. The curly coats of dogs like poodles and Portuguese water dogs are like Velcro around burrs and foxtails. Consider your dog's comfort and your sanity by giving him a "trail trim," especially for summer hiking.

Mosquitoes. Some of the hikes in this book will take you into mosquito territory at certain times of year. Since mosquitoes carry heartworm, it is a good idea to ask your veterinarian about preventative heartworm medication.

West Nile virus has surfaced in some parts of Central California but doesn't seem to pose any significant risks to dogs. A solution of Avon's Skin-So-Soft bath oil in water (half and half) or a eucalyptus compound is less toxic than chemical repellents for dogs.

Ticks. Springtime in coastal areas sparks the bloom of wildflowers as well as annoying little blood-sucking ticks. These teeny, six-legged,

Bumblebee in Rangers Buttons flower

micro spider look-alikes seem to hang around in low brush waiting to pole-vault off the branches and grasses onto hikers' frocks and bare skin or dogs' coats, where they eventually attach themselves to the skin and sink their straws for a drink of fresh blood. They seem especially fond of front leg pits, ears, and inside the fleshy hind legs. Once they become engorged with blood, they drop off satiated and inebriated.

Lyme disease is the fear with ticks. First line of defense is tick repellent in the form of a chemically treated collar much like a flea collar or a topical monthly application of a repellent, some of which have dual purposes (flea and tick). Tick and flea baths are also effective to control the nuisance and minimize the discomfort to your dog. Brushing your dog after a hike prevents the little creatures from making themselves at home.

Persistent scratching or chewing may indicate a tick or a fleabite. A tick bite will have a swollen reddened area where the head has begun to dig into the skin. To help loosen the tick's grip, rub the body of the tick counterclockwise and apply Vaseline or soapy water to the tick. Use tweezers for the final extraction.

Foxtails. The foothills and coastal oak–studded landscape is home to foxtail, the pointed, dry seed of grass that can cling and burrow into a dog's coat or be inhaled from the ground by a dog whose nose rules his life. A persistent, violent sneeze may mean foxtail up the nose, whereas recurring head shaking may mean a foxtail in the ear canal. In either case, it is best to see a veterinarian for the removal to avoid the chance

of the grass traveling deeper and causing infection or more serious damage. It is a good idea to frequently check your dog's ears, paws, and coat for loose foxtails during the hike. Give your dog a thorough hands-on examination after a hike to find the culprits that may be camouflaged between the toe hairs or on the underside of the tail. Brushing with a short wire brush usually collects those grasses before they puncture the skin and travel where they can do potential damage to organs.

Poison oak. This three-leaf plant's resin causes skin irritation that can erupt into a nasty, painful rash. Scratching the affected area, clothing, or dog's coat easily spreads the rash. If you're hiking in an area favored by poison oak, wear long pants and long sleeves. Wash your clothes immediately if you suspect contact with poison oak. Apply Tecnu

Lupines grace the trailside.

soap formula to your skin prior to taking a cool shower or bath (hot water will open your pores and facilitate the spread of the resin). If you do not have Tecnu, wiping the exposed areas of your skin with a bleach-dampened cloth or paper towel, or Clorox premoistened towelettes will help remove the resin residue from your skin. Make sure you give pooch a bath before your next cuddle.

Hydration. The need to supply your dog with frequent and sufficient drinking water on the trail can't be overstated. Exuberant dogs can quickly become dehydrated dogs on a hot day with panting as their only and not always sufficient way to cool off. Less fit and overweight dogs dehydrate more quickly. Drinking enough water helps prevent dehydration that can lead to heat stroke. At a minimum, carry eight ounces of water per one hour or 2 miles of hiking. Know your dog and know the conditions of the hike you're planning.

Wildlife and Trail Hazards

Hiking is synonymous with the great outdoors, where trails inevitably bring you closer to and sometimes through the heart of the realm where "wild" things—plant and animal—live and thrive. You and your dog need to be aware of what lives there so you can identify, respect, appreciate, and, if necessary, protect yourself from it.

Snakes. Rattlesnakes are California's only venomous reptiles. A bite from a baby rattler poses a more serious threat because they usually sink their fangs and hang on, which allows the venom to keep flowing into the victim. Baby rattlers are more numerous in springtime and don't always have rattlers to warn unwanted visitors. Watch for sunbathing snakes on rocks in the spring and resting snakes in the shade of brush in the heat of the summer days. Young dogs, old dogs, and small breeds are more at risk of fatal bites. Check on snake avoidance classes in your community to boost your dog's cautionary instincts around snakes.

Mountain lions. These big cats are in a healthy recovery phase in California because of a good food supply, mostly deer. They are generally as keen on avoiding humans as we are they. If you should be so lucky as to spot one of these elusive animals, give it a wide berth so it can go along its merry way without feeling threatened, especially if cubs are nearby. If it needs a little encouragement to move on, make yourself loud and big and don't turn your back on it. Leash your dog before it decides to investigate and annoy kitty or feels a sudden impulse to play hero to protect you.

Hikers catch the attention of this non-poisonous western yellowbelly racer.

Bears. Bear encounters are more likely than attacks in California. Bears are frequently attracted to campgrounds, lured by the smell or habit of food. These bears are usually easily deterred by the noise of clanging pots and human hollering. The more brazen and repeat offenders are relocated or destroyed. It is important to follow the guidelines about storing food and odiferous articles like soap in your own bear-proof canister or in the bear-proof lockers provided in many of the national and state park and forest service campgrounds. Humans, unfortunately, are the source of the problem, not the bears. But the bears pay the ultimate price.

When people say dogs are "bear bait," it usually means a dog chasing or harassing a bear, especially one with cubs, is bound to run back to you with bear in tow when the situation heats up. If you are uncertain about your dog's behavior around bears or any wildlife, a leash is the only insurance against trouble.

Bear encounters on a hike are generally due to a surprise tête-á-tête around a bend or in a berry patch. Make noise, talk, whistle, or sing when hiking on forested or vegetated sections of the trail.

Coyotes. These animals have been as relentlessly persecuted and unfairly maligned as their larger cousin, the wolf. Speaking strictly of California, encounters between domestic pets and coyotes are usually a result of human encroachment on their habitat. In the wild, coyotes are

The golden-mantled ground squirrel looks like a chipmunk.

more interested in rodents than dogs, more often heard than seen, and quite vocal about letting you know you are trespassing on their hunting grounds or too close to a den of pups. They may even escort you past their turf by paralleling your path from a safe distance. Heed the warning, leash your dog, and walk on by.

Skunks. Slow, jostling, bushy tailed critters, skunks will wrap your dog in a stinging stench if they feel threatened by too much curiosity. See sidebar for the shampoo recipe.

Weather reports can change. Get an updated weather report from the ranger station, especially in the High Sierra, where weather is temperamental enough to turn a cotton ball cloud into a thunderstorm and raindrops into snowflakes at a moment's notice. Always pack raingear, a moisture-wicking and wind-resistant layer, and warm hat and gloves. A plastic poncho or an extra large trash bag will help keep your pack and gear dry. If thunderclouds are on the move, avoid lightning strikes by getting down from peaks, out of the water, and off metal (including a metal-framed pack and hiking poles).

Altitude affects temperature, sun intensity, hydration, and exertion. Expect the temperature to drop the higher you climb and a chilly breeze or cold wind if there's still snow on surrounding slopes and peaks. Without the proper protection, the increase in ultraviolet rays, combined with wind and snow reflection, can add up to blistering sunburns. You can dehydrate rapidly at higher elevation. Altitude is a crucial factor to be taken into account when looking at the distance, time, and difficulty of the hikes described. Even hikes described as easy or moderate can be strenuous if you have not acclimated. (You need at least a couple of days of moderate exercise above 6000 feet before your body chemistry can compensate for the decreased oxygen in the air you are breathing.) Everyone's body adapts differently every time. Although the serious symptoms of altitude sickness are more likely above 10,000 feet, where there is a third less oxygen, it is not unusual to experience shortness of breath, headaches, and loss of appetite at lower elevations.

The best way to prevent or minimize altitude malaise is to take it SLLOWE: start **S**low on a **L**evel **L**ow elevation trail, **O**xygenate with deep, slow breaths, drink **W**ater to hydrate, and keep your head **E**levated above your knees when you bend down (the sudden rush of blood will pound your brain into scaloppine at altitude). Dogs are also subject to altitude effects and require acclimation. Watch for uncharacteristic lethargy in your dog and pace yourselves accordingly.

Remember that **H**eat, **E**xertion, **A**ltitude, and **D**ehydration (HEAD) can be a dangerous combination for both of you.

Canine First Aid and Trail Emergencies

No matter how well prepared, conscientious, and responsible you are, there's always a chance of running into trouble in the great outdoors. In the event of a minor injury or more serious medical emergency, the following first-aid treatments will help make your dog more comfortable until you get him veterinary care.

Scrapes, cuts, and wounds. Remove any foreign object, clean the area with 3 percent hydrogen peroxide, apply pressure with a clean gauze for about ten minutes to stop bleeding and allow for clotting. Apply a clean nonstick pad to the wound and wrap (not too tight) with cling wrap. If it's a paw wound, cover the bandage with a bootie or a sock with duct tape on the bottom for a sole.

Muscle soreness. Rest, cold compresses, and buffered Ascriptin (check with your vet about the dosage) will alleviate the problem.

Heatstroke. Without sufficient water and shade, dogs with long, thick coats or dark coats as well as obese dogs are highly susceptible to heatstroke. If your dog begins to appear lethargic and starts to pant excessively, get him in the shade and apply water-soaked (not icy) towels to his head (to cool the brain) and to his chest, abdomen, and paws. If there's a stream or pond nearby, let him stand in it while you gently pour water over him. If you're in dry terrain, wipe his pads with alcohol swabs; evaporation on the hairless surface can have a cooling effect.

Hypothermia. Thin, short-coated dogs have less protection from the cold. If your dog gets overexposed to cold temperatures (cold rainstorm or fluke snowfall), seek shelter, wrap him up in your extra layers, and share your body heat by keeping him snuggled up to you.

Venomous bites. Keep your dog calm, rinse the affected area with warm water, and get to a vet.

Insect bites. Dogs react to a bee sting or spider bite with swelling or itching. If the stinger is still in the skin, use your fingernail or tweezers to scrape the stinger out and away from where it penetrated the skin (if you squeeze the stinger from the top you will inject more toxin). Put a cold compress on the area and use a topical analgesic spray like Benadryl to relieve the itch. Ask your vet about carrying an over-the-counter antihistamine and the proper dosage for your dog in case of an extreme swelling reaction.

Permits, Regulations, and Fees

Whether emphasizing conservation, recreation, education, or multiuse, each public land agency in the United States was created with a primary charter. In the case of national parks, state parks, reserves, and preserves, protecting and preserving the ecological, archaeological, or historical integrity of the territory dictates dog policy. National parks have the strictest dog policy, wherein dogs are only permitted on the paved surfaces (code word for parking lot) and in some campgrounds.

Generally, dogs are not permitted on the trails in national monuments, state parks, reserves, and preserves.

National recreation areas offer broader public "playground" options emphasizing water sports, with some allowances for dogs.

National grasslands are among the newest category of public lands and are astonishingly dog friendly.

Historically, land administered by the U.S. Forest Service and the Bureau of Land Management (BLM) is designated multiuse and dog friendly. In the best case, dogs are trusted under voice control. In the more stringent cases, leashes are required.

Trails managed by city, county, regional, and private boards vary widely in their policies and attitudes toward dogs and user groups, as well as permits and user and access fees.

Although permits are not generally required for day hikes on national forest or wilderness trails, permits are required for camping in the wilderness, with quotas in some heavily used areas.

The Los Padres National Forest has restrictions on campfires during dry months when fire risk is high and requires campfire permits the rest of the time. In the Sierra Nevada, campfires are prohibited in the high country, where wood

A stripe cut in this tree marks the trail.

is scarce and the sparse vegetation is struggling to survive (generally above 10,000 feet but from 9000 feet on some trails).

Rules and regulations, permit policy, and fees on all public lands are subject to review, update, and change without notice, especially where dogs are concerned. Strictly speaking of day hiking, many state parks and regional parks have day-use fees tied to parking. National parks have entrance fees and a variety of fee packages. Contact the ranger station or administrative agency ahead of time to inquire about the current dog policy, permit process, and fees.

Trail Etiquette for You and Pooch

Based on feedback from park rangers and fellow trail users, the following tips help to avoid and correct the most common complaints and pooch peeves:

- Keep your dog under strict voice control or leash to prevent him from barking, disturbing, or chasing after cattle (dogs can be shot for harassing livestock) or wildlife. Wild animals can't afford to be stressed or distressed by human or canine antics. They need all their energy for feeding and surviving.
- Whether you are heading up or down, it's courteous and safer to leash your dog and step well off the trail to yield the right-of-way to other trail users who may not like or are uncomfortable around dogs. It avoids potential conflicts with other hikers, rumbles with other dogs, and accidents with other trail users (cyclists, horseback riders, seniors, and children are vulnerable to injury from rambunctious dogs). Even dog lovers don't consider muddy paw prints a fashion statement.
- Stay on developed trails (shortcuts cause erosion) and observe the posted rules at the trailhead board and along the way.
- Good trail toilet training habits apply to you and your dog. Dig a cat hole 6 to 8 inches deep, 200 feet away from the trail, water, and campsites, and cover it when finished. Carry out toilet paper and hygiene products in a sealed plastic bag. Be aware that on some heavily used trails, it is posted at the trailhead that all solid waste must be packed out.
- Never leave your dog staked out or leashed to a tree unattended in the parking lot, on the trail, or in camp. Even if he isn't causing a disturbance by barking, it's irresponsible and leaves him vulnerable to injury and predators.

- Be considerate by leashing and leading your dog far away enough from the fishing hole so his splashing and swimming won't scare the fish away and annoy the fishermen.

Leave No Trace Outdoor Ethics and Skills

The pressures of growing populations, developed sprawl, and increased recreational use has significantly impacted the health of fragile ecosystems on our public lands—from the parking lots in our national parks to the backcountry trails in our wilderness areas. In our renewed fervor to embrace nature, we could end up loving her to death. If we are to preserve our wildlands and the resources that support its wildlife and rightful inhabitants for future generations to discover and enjoy, we must each do our part now. The Leave No Trace Center for Outdoor Ethics is a nonprofit organization dedicated to educating recreational users on how to enjoy the gift of our wilderness heritage. Following are some guidelines that incorporate Leave No Trace principles to help create awareness and instill better practices:

1. Plan ahead and prepare

Learn about the rules and restrictions for the area you'll be visiting. Hike and camp in small groups for minimum noise and use impact. Trips on weekdays and outside of popular holidays mean less pressure on the land and more enjoyment for you. Use bear-proof storage for your food. Bring plenty of resealable bags and large garbage bags to repackage unused food and pack out your trash. Use GPS, topo maps, and compasses for navigation. And do not disturb or deface the land with cairns, flags, or paint.

2. Travel and camp on durable surfaces

Protect the integrity of the designated trails by walking in the center of the trail, single file, even if it's muddy or wet. The idea is to keep evidence of your passage across the land to a minimum. Cutting off switchbacks damages vegetation, causes erosion, and scars the land.

In pristine trailless areas, look for durable surfaces like rock, sand, gravel, pine needles, snow, or dried grasses to avoid destroying delicate vegetation, often a food source for wildlife. In a group, spread out to avoid creating new trails.

Use already established campsites and avoid setting up camp atop fragile areas. Wear sandals or light footwear to minimize impact around camp.

A grouse along the trail to Kearsarge Pass

3. Dispose of waste properly

Don't bury trash. Pack out what you packed in. Inspect your picnic site and campsite for traces of leftover food, litter, trash, or forgotten gear. Don't hesitate to pick up litter or trash overlooked or dropped by other hikers. Dig a cat hole both for human and dog solid waste. Cover and disguise it, making sure you pack out toilet paper and hygiene products in a resealable bag. Some sensitive or heavily used wilderness areas require that you pack out solid waste. Use only small amounts of biodegradable soap to wash dishes and groom yourself. Carry water 200 feet away from a stream or lake, and spread the gray water around.

4. Leave what you find

Look but don't touch historic or archaeological structures or objects. Leave natural things the way you found them along the trail. Do not build, dig, or change the natural surroundings, including the removal of rocks, plants, or other objects as mementos. And do not introduce non-native species.

5. Minimize campfire impacts

Observe the posted rules that allow or prohibit campfires. Improperly contained fires can have devastating consequences. Cook with a lightweight backpacking stove.

Where fires are permitted, keep it small and within an existing fire ring or pan or mound fire. Use small sticks from the ground that can be broken by hand. Let fires burn to ash, remove all unburned trash including foil and plastic for packing out, and make sure the ashes are completely cold before scattering them away from the campsite.

6. Respect wildlife

Observe wildlife from a distance without approaching or encouraging contact. Keep away during sensitive times, especially rutting, mating, nesting, nursing or raising young, hibernation, or during winter. Don't feed wildlife. It can alter their behavior and damage their health and chances for survival. Leash your dog around wildlife. Store your food and any scented products securely. Use bear-proof canisters in the backcountry or designated bear boxes in developed campgrounds.

7. Be considerate of other visitors

Horses and other pack animals always have the right-of-way. Leash your dog and step off the trail on the downhill side. Let others enjoy their nature experience with the sounds of silence or calls of the wild without intrusion from dog barks, loud voices and music, generators, and campfire sing-alongs. In the backcountry, take breaks and camp away from the trail and other hikers. Assume that anyone out here would have stayed home if they wanted to see and hear their neighbor.

A caterpillar crosses the trail

Your Bark Makes a Difference

Not everyone loves dogs or is in favor of sharing the trail with our fuzzy friends. One inconsiderate, irresponsible, or ignorant dog owner can reflect on all dog owners as well as jeopardize the already tenuous welcome that dogs enjoy on some of our public lands.

On a purely administrative or enforcement level, it's a lot easier and cheaper for policy-makers to say "no dogs" allowed rather than "only dogs with responsible owners." As far as administrators are concerned, having your dog on the trail is a privilege they have the power to revoke at any time. Don't take it for granted. It's in your best interest, and that of all outdoor enthusiasts who want to continue recreating with their dog, to not only set a good example but to also make other dog owners aware when their dog's behavior is breaking a park rule, putting wildlife at risk, or infringing on the enjoyment of others.

A red-tailed hawk perches on a fence near Monterey Bay

If the transgressions stem from inexperience or ignorance, most reasonable people will appreciate the polite, non-provocative reminder from one of their own. If you sense a confrontational tone erupting, don't risk ruining your day with a conflict. Move on and report the incident to a ranger at the next opportunity. Hikers from all over the country and the world who share their outdoor lives with their dogs have a strong unspoken bond that can be effectively used to preserve and expand access to more hiking pleasures, so that the rebel minority do not affect policy that punishes the majority.

Many communities have trail days where volunteers come together for a few hours a couple of times a year to help park crews repair and maintain hiking trails. It's a great opportunity to nurture goodwill and network with other hikers who share their outdoor life with a canine friend.

Our public lands and the joy of hiking in the wide-open, quiet spaces are increasingly under threat of revoked protection from encroachment by intrusive motorized recreation, industrial exploitation, and human ignorance.

We bear the responsibility as both visitors and stewards of the natural kingdom within the boundaries of public lands. If you witness abuse or desecration of any part of the natural environment along your travels, report the activity to a ranger. Stay informed on what is happening locally, statewide, and federally with parks, forests, and open space. And make your voice heard through your local representatives and by supporting one of the many environmental organizations committed to protecting our public lands.

As an adjunct, support your local humane society and animal shelter programs to help promote spay and neuter drives and adoption programs and to reduce pet negligence and abuse through classroom and community education.

How Trails Were Selected

Central California, as defined in this book, covers a territory of approximately 24,000 square miles, encompassing four national forests (Inyo, Los Padres, Sequoia, and Sierra), five wilderness areas (Ansel Adams, Dinkey Creek, Jennie Lakes, John Muir, and Ventana), one national monument (Giant Sequoia), three state parks and beaches (Henry Cowell, Asilomar, and Carmel), several county and regional parks and preserves as well as BLM open space. The fifty-five hikes described in this book are all on developed trails, fifty-four of the trails are managed and maintained by public land agencies on a local, state, or federal level, and one trail is accessed through a private gated community. On the map you will naturally find more hikes clustered in the regions anointed with large expanses of open space and public lands than in the more densely populated urban areas or agricultural communities.

There are more hikes to be enjoyed with your dog than could be compiled and described in this book. For that reason the fifty-five hikes (more than 225 miles of trail) that made the cut had the "best" of some or all of the following characteristics:

- Off leash
- Water source (creek, lake, ocean, pond, river) for dogs to swim, frolic, and cool off)
- Shade
- Easy access from main highways onto mostly paved secondary roads
- Exceptional scenic, natural, geological, historical, educational, or seasonal attributes
- In the case of the state parks, state beaches, and national monuments, just the fact that dogs were allowed on a trail was a rare enough event to justify including it.
- Off-trail perks may include information on additional dog-friendly jaunts in that area and noteworthy places to sleep and eat.

The hikes are mostly short to moderate in distance with a few more challenging treks, a few off the beaten track, and some overnight options. The difficulty of the hike is determined by the exertion factor based on length and steepness of terrain, taking into account the elevation changes and altitude. The selected hikes are intended to satisfy varying degrees of canine exercise appetites and their humans' fitness levels. Shorter and easier route options for the less fit (pups in training or senior or more sedentary pooches because of health restrictions) within the longer more strenuous hikes are described whenever appropriate.

Using This Book

The book divides the hikes into five regions (distinct biomes with microclimates) of Central California: Central Coast, Sierra Foothills, Eastern Sierra Nevada, Western Sierra Nevada, and the Kern Plateau/Western Divide. Every chapter begins with an overview of each geographic region. Hikes are categorized in regional clusters within that geographic pocket.

Distances and elevations were calculated using USGS maps and a GPS unit for maximum accuracy. Nevertheless, it's possible to find that over

Wildflowers in bloom along Gardisky Lake Trail

the years some trails have been slightly rerouted from their original USGS mapping as a result of natural occurrences, like floods, fires, and slides, or changes in ecological policy. When in doubt, trust the beaten path rather than wandering off at the whim of your techno gear.

The Hike Summary Table at the beginning of the book lists the hikes in the order they appear in the book and breaks them down into basic characteristics to help you narrow down the hikes most suitable to you and your dog. Hikes are divided into two distance groups: **Up to 5 miles** and **Over 5 miles**. **Above 6000 feet** gives you a heads-up about the altitude factor. **Fido fitness scale** rates hikes on suitability to help you match the hike to your dog's level of fitness and conditioning, which only you and your veterinarian can evaluate. Limited fitness (L) applies to dogs with health issues, senior dogs, or young dogs whose developing bones and muscles could be stressed on long or strenuous hikes; fit (F) describes hikes for the average, active, healthy dog; extremely fit (X) describes very strenuous or long hikes suitable only for seasoned hiking dogs in tip-top form. Only hikes rated L are suitable for less-fit dogs or offer a shorter or easier trail option. Refer to the information block at the beginning of each hike for more details. In the **Off leash** column, Yes

What a joy to romp off leash!

(Y) indicates dogs are permitted to hike under voice control on the entire trail; Partial (P) indicates that dogs are required to be leashed on parts of the trail. Hikes listed **Cool and wet** have a water source for your dog's play pleasure, *not* his drinking needs. You can expect trees on at least some sections of a hike listed under **Shade.** The **Campground** column indicates that there are developed sites at the trailhead or within 5 miles. **Backpacking** indicates a hike that makes an enjoyable overnight trip and requires a permit.

The information block at the beginning of each hike is an outline to assist you in preparing for the hike.

Round-trip is the total distance of the hike with a notation on whether the hike is a loop (L), semi-loop (SL), or out and back (OB).

Hiking time is based on a 2-mile-per-hour pace taking into account water and snack breaks, pooch swim stops, and Kodak moments. Hikers' pace will vary according to individual fitness levels, pack weight, terrain, and elevation range, especially if the hikes begin above 6000 feet. When hiking uphill, add 1 mile or thirty minutes for every 1000 feet gained in elevation. One way to estimate your average pace per mile on level ground is to time yourself walking around a sports track.

Elevation range is the lowest point to the highest point on the hike (you can visually track it on the elevation profiles), an important factor in helping you anticipate weather (higher means cooler and colder) and the exertion demands (the wider the range between low and high, the more strenuous the hike). This becomes particularly significant on the Sierra Nevada hikes, which are mostly above 6000 feet.

Difficulty rates hikes as Easy, Moderate, Strenuous, or a combination, taking into account distance, terrain, grade, and elevation range. Pay attention to the elevation factor—without sufficient acclimation, hiking above 6000 feet can easily transform a relatively easy hike into a strenuous experience. Remember the principles of SLLOWE. If the hike is particularly suitable for seniors, young dogs still growing into their bodies and conditioning, or dogs with fitness limitations due to health issues, you will see "less fit okay." The less-fit route option will be described separately at the end of Happy Trails.

Season is first determined by accessibility depending on the regional weather, which can mean too much snow or rain during certain months. Although the trail may be accessible year-round, Season will include tips on the preferable months for optimal enjoyment and comfort, influenced by temperature, trail traffic, water sources, seasonal highlights like wildflowers, as well as nuisances like excessive mosquitoes and poison oak.

California has microclimates as well as seasons, which can make some hikes more desirable than others within a 20-mile radius in the same geographic region. On an August afternoon, a hike along the Monterey Bay can be a foggy forty degrees cooler than a hike 20 miles east in sunny but sometimes triple-digit Carmel Valley.

Pleasers and teasers highlight the best and worst of what to expect. Being allowed to gallivant off leash is a top pleaser. The mention of a creek or lake tells you that your dog will have a chance to at least cool off in something wet or dive in for a swim. "Overnight" will appear as a pleaser if the hike destination or a specific point along the way lends itself to a convenient or memorable campout experience. Poison oak, foxtails, and scorching heat always count as teasers.

Maps refer you to the appropriate USGS topographical map or additional local maps.

Information states whether a permit or fees apply to this hike and lists the land management agency to contact for additional and current details about the area, maps, fees, permits, dog policy, parking, campgrounds, as well as up-to-date information about possible restrictions and closures.

Getting there directions originate from the largest and closest community.

On the trail is the hike description beginning with an overview followed by the nitty-gritty route details, including the less-fit route option if applicable.

Off-trail Perks highlight dog-friendly activities to enhance the people/pooch experience. This may include additional jaunts nearby and noteworthy places to eat and sleep, from campgrounds to historic inns.

A Note About Safety

Safety is an important concern in all outdoor activities. No guidebook can alert you to every hazard or anticipate the limitations of every reader. Therefore, the descriptions of roads, trails, routes, and natural features in this book are not representations that a particular place or excursion will be safe for your party. When you follow any of the routes described in this book, you assume responsibility for your own safety. Under normal conditions, such excursions require the usual attention to traffic, road and trail conditions, weather, terrain, the capabilities of your party, and other factors. Keeping informed on current conditions and exercising common sense are the keys to a safe, enjoyable outing.

The Mountaineers Books

PART 2

The Hikes

CENTRAL COAST

These hikes span the coast from Santa Cruz to San Luis Obispo. The landscape, habitat, and scenery are the richest and most diverse of any region in California—and the climate is mostly temperate for year-round hiking. These communities have succeeded in balancing the needs of humans and nature by shouldering developed areas with open space for recreation and habitat with the cooperation of city, county, state, and federal agencies. The coastal hills and valleys abound with grassy oak-canopied trails, and if your dog is the surf and sand kind of pooch, the Monterey Peninsula beaches won't disappoint there either.

With all the pleasures of this outdoor Eden and its sublime scenery also come three of the most common seasonal annoyances: poison oak, foxtails, and ticks. Keep your ears open for warnings from the occasional sunbathing rattlesnake on hotter inland trails. There's always the rare but pungent beachfront seal carcass just waiting for those dogs that can't resist a roll in all things putrid and stenchy.

SANTA CRUZ

1. Pipeline Road

Round-trip: 5.85 miles, OB
Hiking time: 3 hours
Elevation range: 235–610 feet
Difficulty: Easy
Season: Year-round
Pleasers and teasers: It's a treat to hike in a state park with your
    dog, even on leash
Map: USGS Felton
Information: Fee; Henry Cowell Redwoods State Park,
    (831) 335-3174, *www.parks.ca.gov/parkindex/*

Getting there: Take the Highway 9 North turnoff from Highway 1 in
Santa Cruz. Drive 6 miles along the two-lane mountain road to the park
entrance on your right. The day-use parking area is the second right after
the ranger booth.

On the trail: Pipeline Road, one of three trails that allow leashed dogs,
is a paved path that begins behind the gift shop. Don't let the word
"paved" turn you off. Not only are dog owners lucky to find a state park
that allows dogs on a trail, but also this paved trail under a canopy of
redwoods complete with seasonal streams and a lazy river is astonishingly pristine.

Walk to the far end of the parking lot and follow the sign for the
Redwood Grove and Visitor Center. Just across the road you will see a
sign with a hiker and dog on leash with an arrow pointing right. Walk
100 feet and turn left at the yellow fire hydrant onto Pipeline Road. The

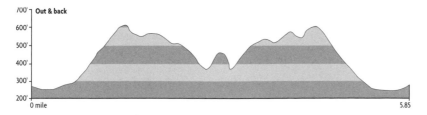

View toward the Pacific Ocean from Pipeline Road

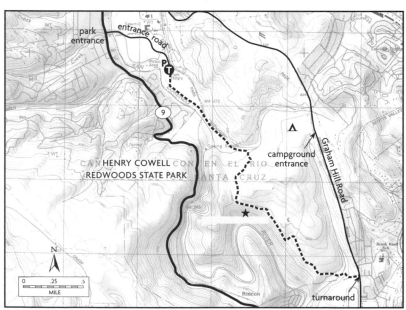

sign on the left side of the trail may not be visible until you make the left turn.

Pipeline Road accommodates hikers with dogs, infrequent park ranger vehicles, and cyclists. The first mile meanders above the San Lorenzo River, whose summer trickle can morph into a torrent following a winter storm. Be prepared for an aerobic workout as the path winds uphill, occasionally steeply, before cresting at a scenic overview and bench at 1.5 miles. On a clear day, you can see all the way to the Santa Cruz boardwalk and the white sand beaches of Monterey across the bay. Be aware that the redwood needles and other forest debris can make the trail especially slippery on the downhill slopes. The path continues undulating approximately 1.5 miles to where it meets Graham Hill Road at the gated southern boundary of the park. Turn around at the gate and retrace your steps to the parking lot.

MONTEREY

2. Skyline Nature Trail to Jacks Peak

Round-trip: 1.24 miles, SL
Hiking time: 1 hour
Elevation range: 854–1045 feet
Difficulty: Easy, less fit okay
Season: Year-round; foggy and cooler summer, clear and warmer fall
Pleasers and teasers: Shade, stunning views; poison oak, leashes
Maps: USGS Monterey, USGS Seaside
Information: Fee; Monterey County Parks, (888) 588-2267,
 www.co.monterey.ca.us/parks

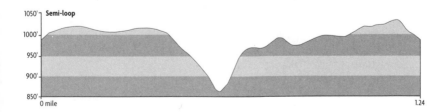

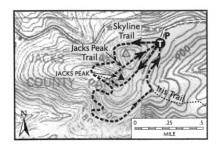

Getting there: From Highway 1 in Monterey, take the Monterey–Salinas Highway 68 East exit, and drive 0.5 mile to Olmstead Road, across from Monterey airport. Turn right and drive 1 mile to Jacks Peak Drive. Take a left on Jacks Peak Drive, and drive 1.5 miles to the entrance and ranger booth. If the ranger is not in the booth, place the fee in the envelope provided at the entrance. Turn right past the booth and follow signs for Talcott Bates Grove and picnic area. Drive 0.5 mile to the parking lot.

On the trail: Although dogs must be on leash in this park, this hike remains one of the most enjoyable and easy jaunts in Monterey. On a clear day, the views are unbeatable, and as far as pooch is concerned, leash or no leash, a pine forest is a cafeteria of smells no dog wants to miss.

The trailhead is at the far end of the parking lot and to the left of the information board. Follow the signs for the Skyline Nature Trail, which is mostly cushioned with Monterey pine needles. Just a few steps into your hike, the Monterey Bay comes into view in its entire splendor. A bird's-eye-view map of the trail identifies the various landmarks of the bay below you, and the bench on the left invites you to sit and soak in this real-life painting.

The geological exhibit at number 4 takes you up close and personal with fossils in the exposed shale walls. Continue along Skyline Ridge,

Trailhead of the Skyline Nature Trail

down the wooden steps, past the left spur trail that goes to Jacks Peak. The views now open southward toward Carmel State Beach, the mouth of the Carmel River, and the green finger of land and rock called Point Lobos. The trail veers left along Skyline Ridge, exposing eastward views up the Carmel Valley. Watch your footing over the tentacle roots of massive, old Monterey pine trunks.

In the spring and early summer, the orange-flowering bushes, known as sticky monkey, grow quite happily along this trail and down the slopes.

The trail switchbacks downward and levels as you approach the Iris Trail intersection. Turn left on Iris Trail, following the signs back to the parking lot.

Back in the parking lot and to your left is a sign with an arrow pointing to Jacks Peak Trail. Walk past a metal barrier across the service road and up Jacks Peak Trail for a short and gentle 0.25-mile spurt to the flat meadow, Jacks Peak, and the highest point on the Monterey Peninsula. The long metal bench on the top faces a clearing that frames the view of Point Lobos.

With your back to the trail you walked, turn right to loop to the parking lot along this wide shale path. If you take the left trail, you will rejoin the Skyline Nature Trail partway down and can follow it in either direction back to the parking lot.

3. Huckleberry Hill Loop

Round-trip: 1.88 miles, SL
Hiking time: 1 hour
Elevation range: 407–715 feet
Difficulty: Moderate, except for one steep stretch of 186 steps
Season: Year-round; foggy and cooler summer, clear and warmer fall
Pleasers and teasers: Off leash, shade, bay views, unique camp-
   ground location; poison oak
Map: USGS Monterey
Information: Monterey City Recreation Department,
   (831) 646-3866, *www.monterey.org/rec*

Getting there: From Monterey, drive 2 miles south along Highway 1 to the Highway 68/Pebble Beach exit and turn right onto Holman High-

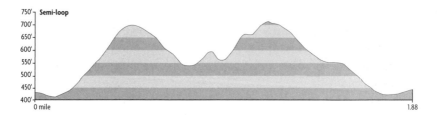

way 68. Drive 1.5 miles and turn right on Skyline Forest Drive to the T intersection. Turn left at Skyline Forest Drive, and drive 2 miles to the entrance of Veterans Memorial Park. Parking for the Huckleberry Hill Loop trailhead is on the left as you enter.

On the trail: This little 81-acre nature gem is tucked above the city of Monterey within hearing and walking distance of the barking seals and other bayside attractions. This short but invigorating hike takes you along a perimeter loop of the Monterey Pine Preserve, one of the largest remaining in the world. A campground, a residential area, the Monterey Presidio, and Highway 68 shoulder the preserve.

Follow the trail along the residential wooden fence, turn left at the Presidio fence onto Presidio View Trail, and hike up 186 wooden steps, which your dog won't even notice because he's in sniff-and-saunter mode by now. Although several of the trails in the preserve are called roads, all are pedestrian only and have a dirt or pine needle base. Presidio View

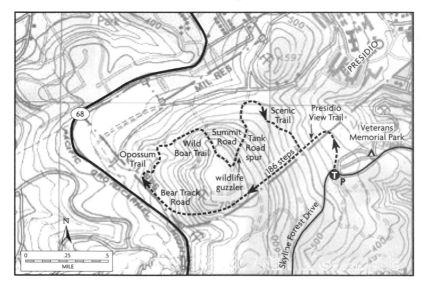

Information signs at the Huckleberry Hill Loop trailhead

Trail crests before dropping down the backside of the preserve toward Highway 68. The increase in traffic noise will be your cue to leash your dog, as a safety precaution, as you approach and get past the few yards of not-so-secure fenceline bordering Highway 68.

Follow Bear Track Road, paralleling Highway 68, until it dead-ends at another Presidio gate. Turn right at the gate and sign for Scenic and Opossum trails. Just a few steps uphill is the sign for Opossum Trail on the left, a much-narrower and more-primitive trail calling on your dog's athletic skills as he threads around trees and leaps over logs. Follow undulating Opossum Trail and turn right where it intersects another road-width, unmarked trail. Turn left onto Wild Boar Trail a short distance ahead. Wild Boar meanders up to a knoll overlooking Monterey Bay's coastal panorama.

Turn right and continue up your last hill onto Summit Road and turn left downhill past the wildlife guzzler (a shallow plastic tub that catches and stores rainwater for animals to drink during the dry season) before your next hit of Monterey Bay views, Del Monte Beach, and Fremont Peak. Continue downhill past the Tank Road spur until you reach a sign for Scenic Trail on your right. Follow the fence and bear left on Scenic Trail to the Presidio View Trail junction near the bottom of the wooden steps. Turn left and downhill toward the campground and the parking lot.

Off-trail Perks

Veterans Memorial Park campground is the only campground within walking distance of downtown Monterey (thirty minutes) and dog-friendly Del Monte Beach (forty minutes). (831) 646-3865

4. Monterey Bay Coastal Recreational Trail to Asilomar State Beach

Round-trip: 8.15 miles, OB
Hiking time: 4 hours
Elevation range: 0–46 feet
Difficulty: Easy, less fit okay
Season: Year-round; foggy and cooler summer, clear and warmer fall, raingear recommended for winter hiking
Pleasers and teasers: Off-leash body surfing at Asilomar State Beach, ocean, views; trail meanders next to road
Map: USGS Monterey
Information: Monterey City Recreation Department, (831) 646-3866, *www.monterey.org/rec;* Pacific Grove Recreation Department, (831) 648-5730

Getting there: From the Highway 1 exit in Monterey, turn right onto Aguajito Road toward the bay. Follow Aguajito Road to Del Monte Avenue and turn left. Drive 1.5 miles on Del Monte Avenue, following signs for the Monterey Bay Aquarium and Cannery Row. Del Monte Avenue becomes Lighthouse Avenue on the other side of the tunnel. Turn right at David Avenue and drive 0.1 mile to where it becomes Cannery Row. The trailhead is on the corner just above the aquarium. There are free parking spaces on side streets, or park in one of the surrounding public parking lots or garages.

On the trail: Although dogs must be on leash until you reach Asilomar State Beach, this flat coastline trail with stunning scenery, tide pools, beaches, and picnic sites is a gem worth sharing with pooch for as short or long a hike as he's up to.

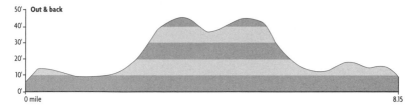

Start on the corner of Wave Street and Cannery Row, just above the Monterey Bay Aquarium. The paved section of the recreational trail is 18 miles long between Castroville (north) and Pacific Grove's Lovers Point Park (at the southern end). From the trailhead to Lovers Point Park, you will be sharing the last paved mile of this popular rails-to-trails project with other walkers and dogs, runners, cyclists, and rollerbladers. The last 3 miles of the hike follow a narrow dirt trail skirting the shoreline of the Monterey Bay Marine Sanctuary to Asilomar State Beach.

The sign on the right welcomes you to Pacific Grove, the monarch butterfly capital. In the spring, much of the coastal trail is adorned by carpets of pink flowers and migrating monarchs, and several of the small beaches along the rocky shore below are blanketed with the protected seals and their young, while sea otters bob in the kelp beds offshore. The Victorian architecture that lines Ocean View Boulevard above the trail and the story-telling murals of Pacific Grove's history along sections of the trail are an unusual but interesting perk for hikers.

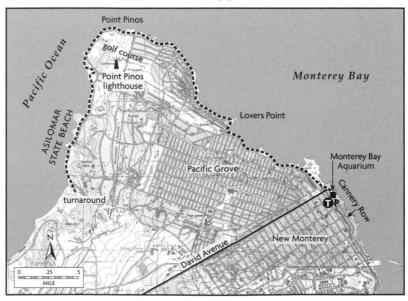

Alex and friend cavorting on Asilomar State Beach

At Lovers Point Park, pick up the dirt trail etching the rugged shoreline. Occasionally, the trail may be diverted around the seawall onto the bicycle lane for a few steps. As your trail bends around the shore, you will spot the verdant plateau of the Pacific Grove Municipal Golf Course and Crespi Pond. On the rise at the far end of the golf course, the little white Point Pinos lighthouse is a romantic reminder of the peninsula's seafaring roots.

The coastline beyond Point Pinos becomes more windswept where the trail officially transitions into Asilomar State Beach. Along a more defined path, crossing boardwalks and negotiating wooden steps, the trail weaves between bouldered coves passing a lovely trellised gazebo ideally set for a picnic lunch overlooking the Pacific.

Your seaside trek ends about 1 mile ahead on the sands of Asilomar State Beach at the edge of the Spanish Bay Golf Links in Pebble Beach. Here, pooch can gallivant and socialize safely off leash where dogs, sunbathers, and surfers frolic.

When pooch and you are sun and surfed out, snap on the leash and retrace your steps.

If you wish to extend your hike, walk to the south end of the beach, where the boardwalk connects Asilomar State Beach to the Spanish Bay parking lot and the trailhead for Hike 5, Spanish Bay to Bird Rock.

PACIFIC GROVE

5. Spanish Bay to Bird Rock

Round-trip: 4.6 miles, OB
Hiking time: 2.5–3 hours
Elevation range: 0–28 feet
Difficulty: Easy, less fit okay
Season: Year-round; foggy and cooler in summer, clear and warmer in fall, raingear recommended for winter hiking
Pleasers and teasers: Off-leash body surfing at Asilomar State Beach, ocean, views; trail meanders next to the road
Maps: USGS Monterey, Pebble Beach Nature Trails, Del Monte Forest Hiking and Equestrian Trails
Information: Fee; Pebble Beach Architectural Review Office, (831) 625-8455, Monday–Friday; The Pebble Beach Riding and Trails Association, Box 154, Pebble Beach, CA 93953

Getting there: For free parking, from Highway 1 in Monterey, take the Highway 68 West/Pacific Grove/Pebble Beach exit south of Monterey. Turn right onto Holman Highway 68. Bear left at Sunset Drive all the way to Asilomar State Beach and park on the left side of the road. This happens to be the end of Hike 4. Walk south across the beach to the boardwalk leading to the Spanish Bay parking lot. The Bird Rock Trail begins at the south end of this parking lot, as indicated by the Point Joe and Bird Rock trailhead sign.

If you prefer parking at the trailhead, follow the directions to Sunset Drive and turn left at Seventeen Mile Drive and the Spanish Bay gated fee entrance to Pebble Beach. Follow Seventeen Mile Drive to the first beach-side parking lot. After your hike, get your money's worth and enjoy driving the coastal section of the famous Seventeen Mile Drive to the Carmel gate and drop down to the dog-friendly beach for another romp (see Hike 6).

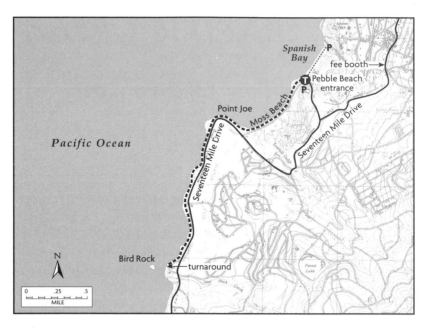

Saorla running along the Bird Rock trail

On the trail: This is a pleasant stroll that mostly parallels the coastal segment of the famous Seventeen Mile Drive, with several opportunities to drop down to small beaches and tide pools on the way to Bird Rock. Leashes are of special importance along the stretches that kiss the road. Bird Rock, a favorite hangout for seabirds and sea lions, is just past the restroom and parking area. Retrace your steps for the return.

6. Carmel Beach

Round-trip: 2.33 miles, OB
Hiking time: 1.5 hours
Elevation range: 0–50 feet
Difficulty: Easy, less fit okay
Season: Year-round; foggy and cooler summer, clear and warmer fall
Pleasers and teasers: Off leash on the Mother of all dog beaches, ocean; occasional seal carcass with maximum "stench" appeal for dogs who can't resist a roll
Map: USGS Monterey
Information: City of Carmel-By-The-Sea, (831) 620-2000

Getting there: From Monterey, drive 3.5 miles south along Highway 1 to Ocean Avenue in Carmel-By-The-Sea. Turn right and drive 1 mile to the beach parking lot at the bottom of Ocean Avenue.

On the trail: This is dog country—local and visiting canines of all ages, sizes, and breeds romp and play from dawn to dusk all week long. Just follow your dog down the sand dune to the water's edge. You can begin your walk along the edge of the Pebble Beach Golf Course to the right, or walk left to the last staircase at the south end of the beach.

Dog walker on Carmel Beach

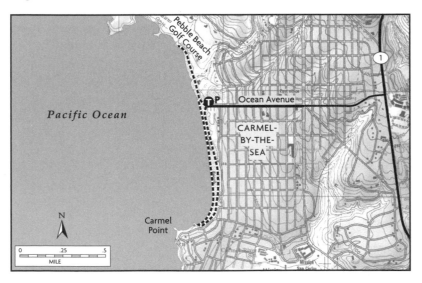

From the south end of the beach, you have the option of walking back along the beach (off leash) or climbing the stairs and returning along the bluff trail (on leash). The second to the last stairway from the south end of the beach has a dog water faucet. (The water is turned off in times of drought for conservation.)

Opposite: Carmel Beach is very dog friendly.

7. Carmel Meadows

Round-trip: 1.74 miles, SL
Hiking time: 1 hour
Elevation range: 23–101 feet
Difficulty: Easy, less fit okay
Season: Year-round; wildflowers in spring, foggy and cooler
  summer, clear and warmer fall
Pleasers and teasers: A state park that allows dogs on the trail,
  ocean; leash law enforced
Map: USGS Monterey
Information: Carmel River State Beach, (831) 649-2836,
  www.parks.ca.gov/parkindex

Getting there: From Monterey, drive 6.2 miles south along Highway 1. Prepare to make a sharp right turn into a small parking area in front of the two-story, oceanfront Bay School just past the Ribera Road turnoff. Additional but less-desirable parking is available along busy Highway 1.

On the trail: This spectacular setting between the Pacific Ocean and the mouth of the Carmel River has plenty of sights and smells to thrill any dog even at the end of a leash.

The trailhead is just at the end of the parking lot between the Bay School and a large meadow with a eucalyptus grove. The crescent-shaped beach behind you is Monastery Beach, where the sandy bottom plunges abruptly into the depths of the Monterey Marine Canyon, making it too hazardous for swimming. The first mile of this hike follows an idyllic coastline of rock outcroppings, teal-colored tide pools, and glistening sandy beaches on the left, with views across to Point Lobos State Reserve, where dogs aren't permitted even as passengers in the car. Point Lobos and its seasonal drapes of fog, craggy coves, and moss-garlanded trees was the

Enjoying the view across Carmel Bay to Point Lobos

inspiration for Robert Louis Stevenson's *Treasure Island*. Enjoy the view because this is as close as you'll get to the reserve with your dog.

A retractable leash can give your dog the illusion of freedom while retaining the control that rangers expect in order to protect the plants and wildlife that make this diverse biome home. What you'll save in fines, you can spend on a patio lunch with pooch later.

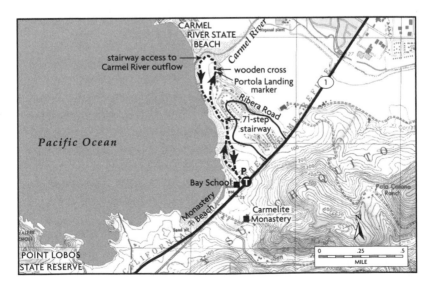

As you approach the residential area that shoulders the park, notice the wide wooden stairway to the right of the first home. This is the stairway you will climb to the upper meadow to complete your loop on the return.

Just past the residences, the trail forks. Bear right away from the beach and follow the trail where it rises past a freestanding stone marking the site where the Spanish explorer Portola and his expedition landed in 1769. Continue uphill to the wooden cross that overlooks the Carmel River and the lagoon where the river breaches the sandbar and pours into Monterey Bay during the winter months. This necessary natural event allows steelhead to swim upriver to their spawning grounds. Breathe in the 360-degree panorama to Pebble Beach in the north, the hills of Carmel Valley to the east, and the dramatic coastline stretching west and south. On a lucky day you might see herons, egrets, and ducks in the lagoon or seals, otters, and spouting whales on the western horizon. For a touch of countryside ambiance, the sheep at Clint Eastwood's Mission Ranch Inn across the lagoon might be grazing in the meadow.

Continue past the wooden cross, tracing the edge of the lagoon where a wooden stairway accesses the beach at the Carmel River outflow. Dogs,

In spring and summer, flowers abound along the Carmel Meadows trail.

on leash, are permitted on the entire stretch of the Carmel River State Beach year-round. The trail back is a service road above the shoreline. Hang on to your leash here because the cottontails think it's good sport to dart back and forth across the trail tormenting visiting dogs.

The trail merges with the main trail you started on. Turn left and up the seventy-one terraced steps just past the sentinel of mega-homes. Turn right at the top of the stairs and follow the bluff trail along the meadow and back down to the main trail and parking area.

8. Mission Trail Loop

Round-trip: 1.43 miles, L
Hiking time: 1 hour
Elevation range: 36–230 feet
Difficulty: Easy, less-fit route option
Season: Year-round; spring brings green grass, seasonal stream, wildflowers
Pleasers and teasers: Off leash
Map: USGS Monterey
Information: City of Carmel-By-The-Sea, (831) 620-2000

Getting there: From Monterey, drive 4.8 miles south along Highway 1. Turn right at the traffic signal onto Rio Road. Drive 0.5 mile and park on the shoulder at the Mission Trail Nature Preserve trailhead across the road from the Carmel Mission. Limited parking.

On the trail: Take a doggie-doo bag provided in the dispenser as you enter the park. There are several garbage cans along the way for disposal. You enter the park on a wide-open, crushed granite base trail that bisects the preserve and leads you to the other entrance along mostly flat terrain

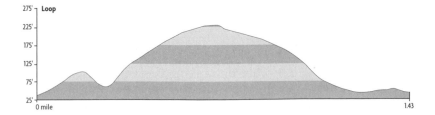

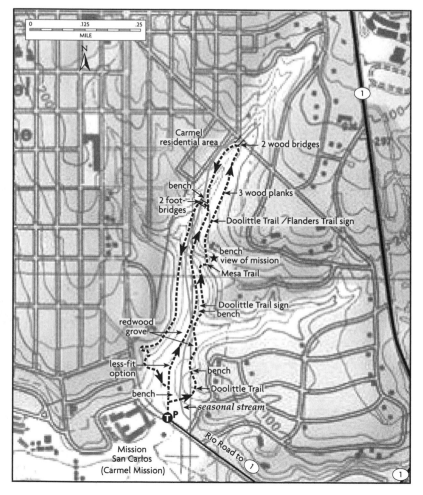

with a gentle incline transitioning to a soft, wood chip base, 0.75 mile past the redwoods. The narrower perimeter trails intersect and merge with the main trail from time to time, undulating along a slope to make it a tad more challenging for exuberant doggies and their owners.

Turn right onto Doolittle Trail at the bench as soon you enter the park across a narrow ribbon of seasonal runoff. Follow the trail as it ascends and winds left paralleling the main trail below. The trail is lined with wild blackberry vines, ivy, and a stand of century plants.

Watch for a peek of the mission's steeple above the trees just as this short, pleasantly meandering trail drops down below a canopy of oaks and soon descends into a grove of redwoods on your left. The slow,

View of the Carmel Mission

narrow seasonal stream trickles over a concrete culvert where the Doolittle Trail briefly merges into the main trail. Make a right at the bench and the sign for the continuation of the Doolittle Trail, which parallels the main trail to yet another bench on the ridge. As you switchback for the third time, you will see a large flattop house at the far edge of a grassy mesa, and just when it looks like you are about to hike right into their backyard, the trail veers left and levels toward the ideal biscuit break and Kodak moment bench on this hike.

The coastline views are probably much the same as they appeared to the Spaniards in 1770 when the Carmel Mission was established. Follow the trail past the Mesa Trail sign to the Doolittle and Flanders trails sign, where you will turn uphill. Watch your footing over the roots that criss-cross the narrow trail. The trail divides soon after walking across the three wooden planks. Stay on the right trail, continuing up a steeper stretch and across a service road. The trail levels out briefly before sloping toward a wooden bridge on the main trail. A right turn over the two bridges spanning the canyon takes you into Carmel's residential neighborhood a few steps above downtown.

To complete the loop, turn left onto the main trail away from the bridges. The downward sweep of the trail combined with the pungent aroma of moist wood chips sends dogs barreling along the lush ravine.

Turn right at the bench and walk across two small footbridges. Turn left down the green corridor and continue to the left cutoff that merges into the main trail. Turn right toward the parking area. Leash your dog as you approach the Rio Road traffic.

Less-fit route option: Stay on the main trail for the first 0.4 mile past the redwood grove on your right. Turn left at the bench and across the two wooden footbridges. Loop left along this green corridor until the trail offers a left cutoff back to the main trail. Rio Road and the parking area will be to your right. The total mileage for this option is 0.8 mile.

Off-trail Perks

If you're hiking around Carmel, consider a side trip into downtown Carmel-By-The-Sea for lunch on The Village Corner Bistro patio, followed by a stroll on Carmel Beach and a luxurious night at Doris Day's Cypress Inn. R. G. Burgers' outdoor patio at the Crossroads Shopping Center at Highway 1 and Rio Road is also a good pit stop for meat eaters and vegetarians.

SALINAS

9. El Toro Creek–Skyline Road Loop

Round-trip: 6.01 miles, L
Hiking time: 3 hours
Elevation range: 154–788 feet
Difficulty: Moderate, less-fit route option
Season: Year-round; wildflowers in the spring, hot and exposed
   slopes in summer
Pleasers and teasers: Off leash, views; ticks in spring and summer,
   grazing sheep in spring, foxtails in summer and fall
Map: USGS Spreckels
Information: Bureau of Land Management, (831) 394-8314,
   www.ca.blm.gov

Getting there: From Highway 1 in Monterey, take the Monterey–Salinas Highway 68 East exit and drive 11 miles toward Salinas. You will see a residential development on your left with a fence separating the housing development from the parking area. Make a careful left (you have to cross a lane of oncoming traffic) into the long dirt parking area facing the Toro Estates residential area behind the fence.

On the trail: Until 1990, these 7200 acres comprised Fort Ord Military Reservation, enclosed by Highway 68, Highway 1, and Reservation Road. BLM public lands are historically among the most rugged and remote of our recreational areas and rarely considered scenic. If there's an exception to that rule, this hike is it. This chunk of BLM land is a stellar example

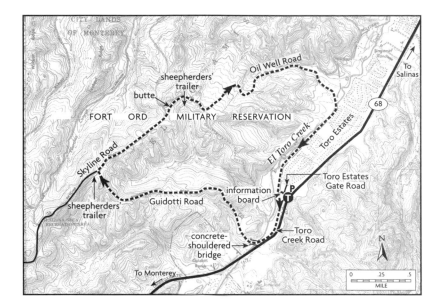

of the successful conversion from military use to recreational use and restoration of wildlife habitat crowned by a spectacular setting.

The trailhead is to the left of the parking area and residential homes. Walk through the opening in the fence past the information board that usually has maps of the trails you will share with mountain bikes and horses.

Facing the large information board, follow the double-track trail in the center, Toro Estates Gate Road. Notice that many of the trails are called "roads," a legacy from Fort Ord days when many of these dirt trails were jeep roads lacing the landscape.

At the trail intersection of Toro Estates Gate Road and Toro Creek Road, turn left onto Toro Creek Road. Follow Toro Creek Road, a sandy trail that parallels noisy Highway 68 on your left and the creek bed on your right. It's a good idea to keep your dog on leash as long as you can see the cars whizzing along Highway 68. Toro Creek Road becomes Guidotti Road just before the trail veers right away from Highway 68. Cross the concrete-shouldered bridge, built in 1911, spanning El Toro Creek.

Across the bridge, bear right on the double-track that stretches up and down, leveling briefly over the next 0.25 mile before reaching the ridge. Snap off the leash—time to party! The vistas across the oak canyons and greening hills from winter rains is a treat for the eyes and a safe, boundless playground for your dog. The fertile Salinas Valley lays to the east with

Mount Toro rising behind you; the Carmel Valley hills are to the west.

Between March and June, expect to catch a glimpse of 400 to 800 grazing sheep on the surrounding hillsides. The sheep enhance this hike with an enchantingly bucolic ambiance, while at the same time requiring added diligence and respect on the part of dog owners and a dog with good impulse control. Off-leash dogs are known to have caused severe to fatal injuries to sheep, which can also inflict serious injury to a dog in their attempt to self-defend. A leash is the only sure way to keep the sheep and dogs apart until you have walked a safe distance from the flock.

Turn right at the intersection of Guidotti Road and Skyline Road, just past a turnout at the sheepherders' seasonal camp. The trail sign at this intersection has a small plaque marking the San Juan Bautista Historic Trail, illustrated with a Spaniard on horseback led by a Native American on foot.

Fremont Peak rises on the northeastern horizon; the Monterey Bay stretches to the northwest. Keep your eye out for more flocks on the knolls ahead and be prepared to snap on the leash for safe passage through bah-bah land.

The rolling descent along Skyline Road continues to a fork at a butte. Stay on the trail to the right of the butte where the trail becomes Oil Well

Keep your dog on leash if sheep are present along the El Toro Creek Trail.

Road, a gradual, sinewy final descent to the flatlands. The trail eventually drops in the cleavage of the bosomy seasonal riparian habitat. Turn right on Toro Creek Road to complete your loop with the Toro Estates neighborhood now in view. Cross El Toro Creek at its narrowest and mostly dry point just across from the school playground.

Eucalyptus groves and patches of wild poppies soften the transition between manicured civilization and wilder grasslands. Expect more family traffic on this stretch of flat trail, particularly on weekends. Turn left on Toro Estates Gate Road, go past the residential compound and back to the parking lot.

Less-fit route option: This route traces the perimeter of the fenced residential neighborhood on two sides. Enjoy an easy 1-mile out and back by following Toro Estates Gate Road along the fence and turn right onto Toro Creek Road between the creek and the east perimeter of the neighborhood. This is the last half-mile section on the return of the main hike.

10. Ollason Trail to Simas Peak

Round-trip: 12.3 miles, SL
Hiking time: 7 hours
Elevation range: 184–2245 feet
Difficulty: Strenuous, less-fit route options
Season: Year-round; best climate and landscape in winter, spring, and fall; hot, dry summers
Map: USGS Spreckels
Pleasers and teasers: Partial off leash; minimal shade, hot and dry exposed ridges, foxtails in the summer
Information: Fee; Monterey County Parks, (831) 484-1108, *www.co.monterey.ca.us/parks/*

Getting there: From Highway 1 in Monterey, take the Monterey–Salinas Highway 68 East exit toward Salinas. Drive 12 miles along Highway 68, and exit at Portola Drive. Turn right at the stop sign to park entrance.

On the trail: Toro County Park's almost 5000 acres includes more than 20 miles of hiking, biking, and horseback riding trails, with playgrounds and developed picnic areas for total family fun.

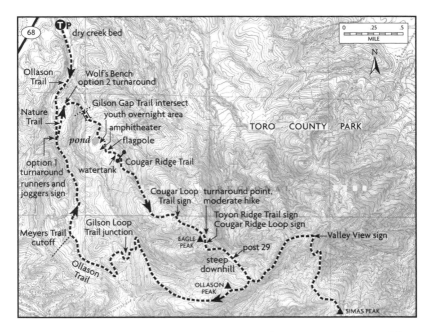

Like most parks on the Monterey Peninsula, Toro is made up of for-mer ranchland parcels, and many of the trails were once dirt tracks that ranchers used to run cattle, check fencelines, and patrol their land on horseback or in pick-ups. Seasonal cattle grazing, water troughs, and an old windmill are some of the remaining evidence of this park's ranch-ing legacy.

Just past the park entrance, a board with a map of the area outlines the trails and picnic areas. Maps are usually available at the park entrance booth. Toro doesn't have well-marked trails. At some trailheads and trail intersections, do not expect much more than a post indicating if this is a hiker, equestrian, or biking trail and an arrow pointing you in the trail's direction. The good news is that this hike and its shorter option are easy to track and fairly well marked.

Drive past the entrance along the main road and turn right into the second parking lot at the far end, closest to the bathroom building and the children's play set.

Pick up the unmarked Ollason Trail behind the public bathroom building by crossing a usually dry creek bed and turning left to start your merry journey.

This section of Ollason Trail is for hikers only. The trail narrows and remains mostly shaded as you walk deeper into the warming canyon,

trading developed picnic sites and parking lots for eroded sand cliffs above the lush ravine.

Stay on the main trail, passing a windmill on your left. Walk up a few wooden steps as the trail gradually transforms into a narrower footpath, gently rising above the creek bed about 20 feet below you. If this athletic section of the trail doesn't invigorate your dog, then the probable sight and sound of mooing cows in the ravine ahead will surely get his attention—one of the reasons for a leash on this trail.

Cross to the other side of the creek and climb out of the canyon along a wooden bridge and switchback up some wooden stairs to where the hiker's-only section of Ollason Trail merges into the main, multiuse section of the Ollason Trail. Notice the sign directing joggers and runners onto the canyon trail you were just on. If you hike the complete semi-loop, you will be returning from the right on Ollason Trail.

Turn left and continue up and out of the canyon along this wider,

A well-camouflaged horned lizard

leveling trail. Turn right, approaching staff trailers and public bathrooms, onto the short, paved special needs nature trail leading to Wolf's Bench, named after one of the park's benefactors. The cleverly designed educational exhibits describe habitat and inhabitants of the meadow and seasonal tule reed wetlands both in text and in Braille.

Continue past Wolf's Bench, which overlooks the Salinas Valley, up the dirt road to the left of the meadow, and bear right. The wide trail transitions into a narrow, rougher hillside trail before dropping into a grassy meadow and across Gilson Gap Trail and a small bridge. Cross the paved road to the Cougar Ridge trail marker and the youth overnight area. Walk to the left of the pond, between the flagpole and small amphitheater up a narrow, unmarked trail past the tank on your right, through the gate, and up the moderate slope of the rolling grassy hills. At about 3 miles, the views open up to the southeast toward Carmel Valley. The little white dot on the ridge in the distance is the abandoned fire tower above Snivleys Ridge and Garland Ranch Regional Park.

The trail plateaus ahead with views of the bay and the mouth of the Salinas Valley before starting up the steeper stretch of trail past the Cougar Loop Trail sign. If your dog responds well to voice control, he'll love to romp off leash up here, as long as there are no cattle to harass.

Continue along the Cougar Ridge Trail and up a steeper stretch still, to Eagle Peak, and the end of Cougar Ridge Trail. This is a good turnaround point for a moderate hike.

The trail continues right, under the oak canopy, to the Cougar Ridge Loop sign on the right and Toyon Ridge Trail sign on the left. Stay on the grassy track ahead and along the saddle until it emerges from the oak forest and the steep downhill, scrub-lined trail. The trail dips as you pass post number 29 on the right. Continue down past post 29 and along a shaded canyon of moss-dangling oaks, where the trail's S path comes up along a well-worn single-track trail emerging on the ridge bordered by rolling meadows and an eroded ravine on the right and oaks on the left. Follow the single-track trail below the saddle to the trail sign in the swale and turn left toward Simas Peak along the steep, dry stretch of trail. Consider calling it a day at the sign for Valley View at the top of the knoll.

Before you are lured farther along the meandering trail that undulates over a couple of knolls beyond to the 2245-foot Simas Peak, be forewarned that this last mile of hiker-only trail is primitive, hot, dry, eroded, overgrown, and steep.

If you still have plenty of water and you and pooch are summit hungry, follow the trail etched up and down along the spine to the Simas Peak elevation marker.

On the return, retrace your steps back to the swale and the Ollason Loop trail marker. Turn left to go around Ollason Peak and Ollason Trail across the open grasslands and descend into the oak forest. Follow Ollason Trail past Gilson Loop, rustic ranch fences, water troughs, cattle gates, and Meyers Trail cutoff. Although your dog may have energy only for thoughts of a sofa snooze, it's a good idea to leash him before you hear the moos in case he gets a second wind and turns into a herding dog.

Turn left at the joggers and runners sign and follow the shaded canyon trail to the parking lot and picnic grounds, where cool grass awaits your tired tootsies and pounded paws.

Less-fit route options: Option 1: Hike along the flat, shady joggers and runners section of Ollason Trail, from the parking area to the intersection of the main Ollason Trail. Turn around at the intersection. Option 2: Continue out of the canyon onto the special needs paved nature trail and turn around at Wolf's Bench.

CARMEL VALLEY

11. Snivleys Ridge

Round-trip: 5.32 miles, L
Hiking time: 3 hours
Elevation range: 170–1675 feet
Difficulty: Strenuous, less-fit route option
Season: Year-round; spring flowers, seasonal waterfall, exposed ridges can be hot in summer
Pleasers and teasers: Off leash, river, pond, views; poison oak, foxtails in summer and early fall
Maps: USGS Seaside, USGS Mount Carmel
Information: Monterey Peninsula Regional Park District, Garland Ranch Regional Park, (831) 659-4488, *www.mprpd.org/parks /garland.htm*

Getting there: From Monterey drive 4.5 miles south along Highway 1. Turn left at the traffic signal onto Carmel Valley Road and drive 8.5

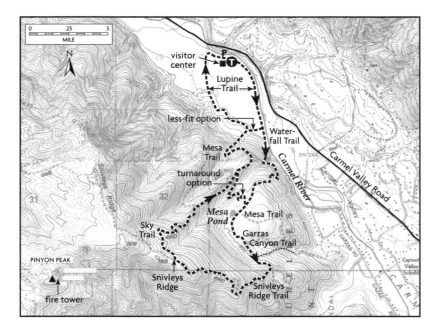

miles east to Garland Ranch Regional Park on your right. The first parking area is off the gravel shoulder to the right. Access to the second and
larger parking lot is just before the park sign. A riverside path connects
both parking lots year-round, and signs direct you from either bridge to
the visitor center on the south side of the Carmel River.

On the trail: Hikers, horseback riders, and cyclists share most of Garland
Park's expansive 4500-acre trail system and diverse terrain. Many a pup
has been initiated to the joy of the trail by romping around the flat, open
meadow while their muscles and stamina grew into the more challenging ridge-top trails. And many are grateful again for the familiar gentle
meadow trails in their senior years. This hike offers a little of everything
for every ability and ambition.

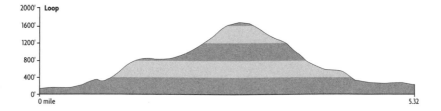

Stopping for water is important on hot, dry summer days.

Pick up a pocket trail map at the visitor center. Walk eastward along Lupine Trail, paralleling the Carmel River on your left and the meadow on your right. At the Y, follow Lupine Trail to the right as it veers away from the river. Bear left and follow the signs to Waterfall Trail as it rises sharply but briefly under a lovely canopy of trees and then levels off, continuing past two more signs to Waterfall Trail and a No Horse sign. Waterfall Trail narrows and dips into the shallow, shaded ravine lined with moss-covered boulders, ferns, and a trickling seasonal creek. As you walk across the wooden footbridge, look up to see moss and vines covering the 120-foot-high rock face, where a seasonal waterfall fed by heavy winter storms tumbles.

Leaving the primeval canyon below, follow the trail as it sweeps up from the base of the waterfall to several stretches of wooden and composite steps. This is a popular and narrow trail where one rambunctious pooch can easily bump hikers off the side. Keep an ear and eye out for dogs bounding down, large roots, and the hallway of low gnarly tree limbs that droop over some sections of the trail.

The views open as you climb and the steepness levels out to a gradual meandering incline under mossy oaks. The trail comes to a horse gate and switchbacks so the valley is on your right. Stay on Waterfall Trail zigzagging your way to the Mesa Trail sign ahead. Follow Mesa Trail to the grassy tabletop overlooking Carmel Valley. The mesa (Spanish for "table") is a destination in itself with drinking water for horses, dogs, and humans; a grassy playground for dogs to spin; a pond to paddle; and a couple of benches to sit on, snack, and breathe in the view. Feel free to call it a day and loop back to the visitor center along the Mesa Trail by backtracking from the pond and turning left at the sign.

For those still up for the top-of-the-ridge rewards, continue along the main trail past the pond following the signs for Garzas Canyon Trail and Snivleys Ridge. Look ahead and above the pond to see Snivleys Ridge, your final destination. The trail veers left past the pond, edging the mesa at the foot of the ridge, passing five majestic oaks and a memorial bench through a sun-dappled, tree-lined corridor before emerging at another trail intersection for Garzas Canyon downhill and Snivleys Ridge uphill. Turn right and follow Snivleys Ridge 0.5 mile up the steep—and at times eroded, dry, and slippery—route with expansive views. This stretch of mostly exposed trail is a hoofer and a tongue hanger. Having four legs is a definite advantage. The trail folds back and forth across the ridge, relentlessly stoking your metabolic furnace. One last push along a narrow, sage-lined stretch and the sight of the fire tower on the highest knob rising left above Snivleys announces you are closing in on your goal. Finally you'll spot an old barbwire fence on the left where the trail winds between the fence posts and past a paddock area on the right. Take a few more steps to the bench for a well-deserved rest and savor the ocean views to the west. Most dogs can't wait to plop down under the bench at this point and couldn't care less about anything else, except a biscuit and water.

When you're ready, follow Sky Trail down the north slope of the ridge overlooking Monterey Bay and the Santa Cruz Mountains on the distant horizon and Mesa Pond down to your right. At the bench where the trail branches, bear right to continue along Sky Trail until it meets Mesa Trail. Turn left onto Mesa Trail to Lupine Trail at the bottom.

Turn left on Lupine Trail and follow it across the meadow to the visitor center and over one of the bridges to the parking lot. While you're thinking "hot shower," pooch is zeroing in on the river for one last cool splash and a shake.

Less-fit route option: Loop around the meadow on the Lupine Trail from the visitor center.

12. Garzas Canyon to Redwood Canyon

Round-trip: 3.67 miles, SL (summer/fall); 3 miles, SL (winter/spring); 4 miles, SL (winter/spring option to Redwoods)
Hiking time: 2 hours
Elevation range: 253–833 feet
Difficulty: Moderate
Season: Year-round; 3.67 mile semi-loop depends on winter rains and footbridges, 3 mile semi-loop alternative has year-round, permanent bridges
Pleasers and teasers: Off leash, creek, shade, views; poison oak
Maps: USGS Carmel Valley, USGS Mount Carmel
Information: Monterey Peninsula Regional Park District, Garland Ranch County Park, (831) 659-4488, *www.mprpd.org/parks /garland.htm*

Getting there: From Monterey, drive 4.5 miles south along Highway 1. Turn left at the traffic signal onto Carmel Valley Road, and drive 10 miles east. Turn right onto Boronda Road. Follow Boronda Road 0.5 mile, and after the one-lane bridge across the Carmel River, make a left onto East Garzas Road. Drive 0.1 mile and park by the trailhead off the road along the fence. There is room for about three to four cars. If it looks crowded, go back 0.1 mile and park in front of the other trailhead.

On the trail: This trail has it all: shade from the oaks, buckeyes, and bay trees; towering redwoods; Kodak-moment swimming holes; six stream crossings with rustic bridges to keep your socks dry; fern meadows; views; and poison oak.

The trail begins with a moderate climb past the sign for River Trail and Garzas Canyon Trail. Follow Garzas Canyon Trail past the Veeder

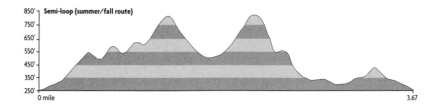

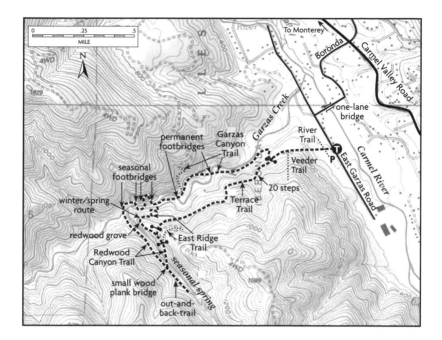

Trail cutoff to your left to the bench and the sign for Terrace Trail about 0.25 mile ahead. Notice the spur trail bending right down the canyon; that's the trail you'll return on to complete your loop in a couple of hours. Follow the narrowing Terrace Trail through a horse gate designed to keep horses off this fragile stretch of trail along mostly level terrain before going down twenty terraced steps. The trail begins to hug the sometimes-steep hillside, snaking along the slope above Garzas Creek, past delicate maidenhair fern gardens, craggy rock walls, and a variety of delicate wildflowers. Pay attention to your footing.

In a couple of bends, the rushing creek below will drown out the echo of Carmel Valley Road, and you won't believe that such a pristine setting could coexist so closely and harmoniously with civilization. The mountain lions, bobcats, deer, and coyotes that make the hills of Garland Ranch Regional Park their home can't believe it either. Just past another horse gate, Terrace Trail intersects East Ridge Trail and the redwoods come into view below. The abandoned fire tower above Garland Park sits up to the west.

If you are hiking this trail during the summer and fall months, turn left on East Ridge Trail past a bench, and then turn right onto the Redwood Canyon Trail. Follow the trail downhill through another gate to a

Garzas Creek, full from the winter rains

small wood plank bridge over a seasonal stream. Turn left onto the spur trail for a worthwhile half-hour out-and-back side trip past giant ferns hanging from rock outcroppings and a seasonal waterfall. The trail ends on a plateau with the boundary marked by a three-foot-round fallen tree. Turn around and go back to the bridge. Turn left to continue among the light-filtering redwoods to Garzas Creek and the first of the four seasonal footbridges zigzagging between the east and west shores of the creek.

Follow the trail along the frothy creek, dotted with water-draped boulders, plush grasses, and crystalline swimming holes waiting for your pooch to paddle and frolic.

Beware of frost or moss that make for slippery bridge crossings. Shortly after the fourth footbridge and through yet another horse gate, Redwood Canyon Trail and East Ridge Trail intersect. Stay on East Ridge Trail and cross the first permanent footbridge and follow the trail along the creek. East Ridge Trail soon merges into Garzas Canyon Trail. Follow the trail to the second permanent footbridge. The creek is now on your left for the last few hundred yards before you start to switchback out of the canyon to the bench and the intersection of the Garzas Canyon and Terrace trails. Catch your breath and turn left down the trail back to your vehicle, where a towel for pooch and Tecnu soap for you will come in handy.

Winter/spring route: During the wetter months, there are two alternate semi-loops. The first is a 3-mile route that bypasses Redwood Canyon because seasonal footbridges have been removed. Turn right on East Ridge Trail at the junction with Terrace Trail, and then turn right at the bottom of the canyon to follow the trail along the creek. Switchback up out of the canyon to Terrace Trail after the second permanent bridge and turn left at the bench and down to the trailhead parking lot.

The second winter/spring route allows you to enjoy the redwoods and adds 1 mile to your hike. Turn left on East Ridge Trail and right on Redwood Canyon Trail, which takes you to the edge of Garzas Creek at the bottom of Redwood Canyon. Since the seasonal footbridge is removed at this time of year, retrace your steps up the canyon and pick up the first winter/spring route option at the East Ridge and Terrace Trail junction.

13. Los Padres Dam to Carmel River Campsite

Round-trip: 9.04 miles, OB

Hiking time: 5–6 hours or overnight at Bluff Camp or Carmel River Camp

Elevation range: 961–1367 feet

Difficulty: Moderate, less-fit route option

Season: Year-round; fall for shallowest river crossings, summers can be hot

Pleasers and teasers: Off leash, river, shade, solitude, good overnight; ticks, poison oak

Map: USGS Carmel Valley and Ventana Cones

Information: Fee; Los Padres National Forest, Monterey Ranger District, (831) 385-5434, find campfire permit information at *www.fs.fed.us/r5/lospadres*

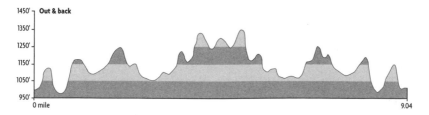

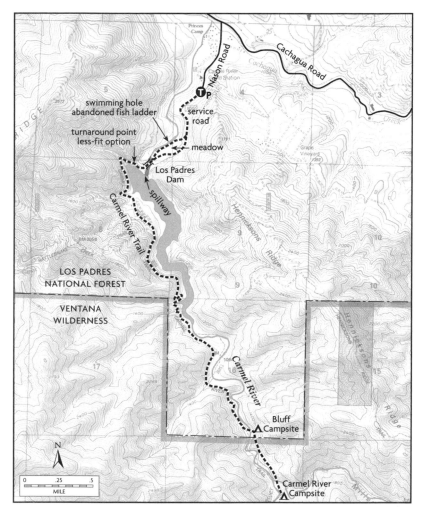

Getting there: From Monterey, drive 4.5 miles south along Highway 1. Turn left at the traffic signal onto Carmel Valley Road, and drive 16 miles east to Cachagua Road. (Carmel Valley Road narrows after the first 13 miles and becomes twisty past Carmel Valley Village.) Make a right turn onto narrow, snaky Cachagua Road and follow it for 5 miles over scenic hill and dale and past vineyards until the road drops down and levels into Cachagua Valley. Turn right onto Nason Road, which deteriorates beyond the Cachagua Community Park. The road ends in a dirt parking area at a chain-link fence just beyond the unmanned ranger station.

Opposite: View toward the Los Padres Dam

On the trail: Walk through the gate. The hike to the dam along the service road used by California American Water Company is one of the easiest places to access Los Padres National Forest. Follow the 0.75-mile dirt road to the dam past two large meadows above the river.

The road drops down to the lower meadow. If you have a water-loving dog, turn right at the fork and follow the road down to the river's edge below the spillway and the abandoned fish ladder to the swimming hole.

To continue toward the dam, go back up the hill to the main road and turn right across the bridge over the spillway. Turn left uphill to the top of the dam. The views up the river canyon are spectacular. Continue right on the uphill trail along the dam. The trail eventually levels off with views back across the Cachagua Valley vineyards and the outline of the service road you walked on from the parking lot. The trail cuts slightly inland, going up and down, with the dam weaving in and out of sight until you find yourself looking back, straight across to the spillway. Eventually the trail narrows and emerges from a corridor of trees at a prominent trail sign with trails going uphill and straight ahead. Stay on Carmel River Trail, straight ahead. The river comes into view as a slithering fluid 100 feet below rock canyon walls and grassy banks. The trail curves and hugs the hillside on the right, which can seem precipitous in some stretches. Pay attention to your footing and leash your dog if you're uncertain of his balance. Harnesses are the ideal dress code for this trail. The trail eventually takes a definite turn downward to the river's edge.

The first body of water at the bottom is a tributary feeding the Carmel River from a canyon on the west side. To continue to Carmel River

Off-trail Perks

There are three outstanding dining and provisioning stops along Carmel Valley Road. Earthbound Farms Produce Stand, one of a handful of organic kitchens in the country, has an assortment of goodies from fresh muffins, salads, and sandwiches to pesticide-free fruit to fill your picnic basket. Farther up the road, at Mid-Valley Shopping Center, Jeffrey's Grill and Catering serves breakfast and lunch on their dog-friendly patio. Deli Treasures' outdoor tables around the corner make a good pit stop for a cup of mouthwatering tomato bisque or a few snacks for your backpack. If you drive through Carmel Valley Village early in the morning and don't mind the line, the Wild Goose Café's morning glory muffins and blueberry scones are worth the wait.

Murphy sniffs a California newt, commonly seen on the trail in the wet season.

Campsite, you must cross this tributary, which, depending on the season, is doable over rocks in your hiking boots or switch to river sandals to cross the potentially knee-high water.

Water-loving dogs can't wait to hurl themselves into the water and paddle to the other side. Others may need to be carried or leashed for a comfortable, safe crossing. If you don't feel like tackling this crossing or the next two, this makes a pleasant turnaround destination.

Otherwise, cross the tributary to the right and pick up the trail on the other side, bearing to the right, behind the fire pit and up around the back of the very large oak tree to follow the trail upward to the ridge. The views open up to the Ventana Wilderness mountain ranges, with intermittent spectacles of century plants clinging to the canyon walls, unusual tree groves growing out of rock outcroppings, delicate ferns, and wildflowers and honeysuckle bushes.

At the point where the river below seems to horseshoe around a bend, the trail switchbacks downhill to the riverbank and a finger of land with two campsites. The water boils and tumbles over the boulders in this narrow stretch. Bluff Campsite consists of a couple of pleasant primitive campsites on a rise just across the river. Except for winter and early spring when the strength and depth of the flow makes it impractical and unsafe to attempt, this is a fairly easy crossing. Walk through Bluff Campsite and follow the trail on the left into the Ventana Wilderness. Carmel River Campsite is about 0.5 mile past Bluff Campsite with just one more river crossing. Carmel River Campsite is a pleasant destination for picnicking, cooling off in the narrow river, or an easy overnight.

Less-fit route option: The relatively flat, 0.75-mile trail (1.5 miles round-trip, out and back) to the dam, with the exception of a couple of moderate ups and downs, provides hikers and their less-fit pooch an opportunity to enjoy quiet, off leash, and open space freedom with backcountry views and minimal to moderate exertion.

BIG SUR

14. Pfeiffer Beach

Round-trip: 0.8 mile, OB
Hiking time: 30 minutes
Elevation range: 0–22 feet
Difficulty: Easy, less fit okay
Season: Year-round; foggy and cooler summer, clear and warmer fall
Pleasers and teasers: It's one of the few dog-friendly beaches south of Carmel, ocean
Map: USGS Pfeiffer Point
Information: Fee; Los Padres National Forest, Monterey Ranger District, (831) 385-5434, *www.fs.fed.us/r5/lospadres*

Getting there: From Monterey, drive 31 miles south on Highway 1. Take the second hard right 0.5 mile past the Big Sur Station and ranger information on your left. Shortly after you start down this one-lane paved road, you will see the large rock sign for

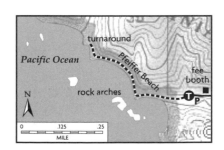

Pfeiffer Beach and the U.S. Forest Service logo. Drive 2 miles to the fee booth and parking lot.

On the trail: The short, sandy trail to the beach is the threshold into a surreal canvas of white sand against a backdrop of wave-sculpted rock arches. This beach's isolated beauty and firmly packed sand combine to create a unique escape where you and your dog can spend anywhere from an hour to a day walking, picnicking, and savoring your good fortune that you can share this pristine, hidden beach together.

Arched rock on Pfeiffer Beach

Off-trail Perks

Stock up on sweet treats and hearty breads from the Big Sur Bakery and Restaurant. If you have time for a coast drive and exploration between Pfeiffer Beach and San Simeon (60 miles to the south), watch for the coastal access and picnic site signs along Highway 1 as well as pleasant forest service campgrounds. Some campgrounds have trailheads heading eastward and uphill into the drier, more remote, and rugged parts of Los Padres National Forest; other trails meander along the bluffs overlooking the Pacific. Elephant Seal Vista Point, 1 mile north of San Simeon, offers a great opportunity to see the protected elephant seals in one of their breeding and nursing grounds during the winter months. Savor the experience and obey the regulations.

SAN LUIS OBISPO

15. East Cuesta Ridge

Round-trip: 7.9 miles, OB
Hiking time: 3.5–4 hours
Elevation range: 1555–2536 feet
Difficulty: Moderate
Season: Year-round; summers can be hot
Pleasers and teasers: Off leash, views; extreme sun exposure in the summer
Map: USGS Lopez Mountain
Information: Los Padres National Forest, Santa Lucia Ranger District, (805) 925-9538, *www.fs.fed.us/r5/lospadres*

Getting there: From San Luis Obispo, drive north 5.5 miles on Highway 101 to the Cuesta Grade Summit, indicated by a sign stating the elevation as 1522 feet. Make a right into the paved truck pullout just a short distance beyond the sign. You will notice a short, narrow road curving above the pullout to a gate; drive up the road and park on the dirt shoulder. You can be fined for parking in the pullout.

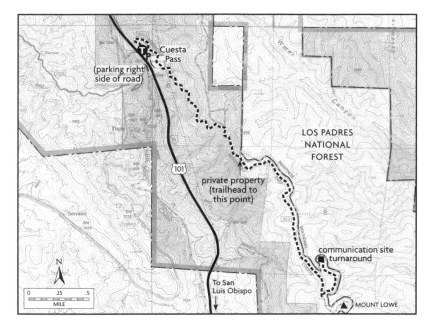

On the trail: The trail to the ridge is actually a well-maintained, little-used dirt and gravel service road leading to several communication towers and Los Padres National Forest trails. The road crosses private property for the first 2 miles before entering Los Padres National Forest for another couple of miles of trail.

The highlight of this hike that winds gradually to a panoramic summit is the open views overlooking San Luis Obispo and the nearby morros (the nine hills belonging to a chain of ancient volcanoes) all the way to the coast.

The hike begins once you are through or over the gate, which may be locked to keep out unauthorized vehicles. Follow the main road that winds uphill for approximately 4 miles. Respect the private property and no trespassing signs meant to keep users on the road and off the surrounding land until you enter forest service property. The noise from Highway

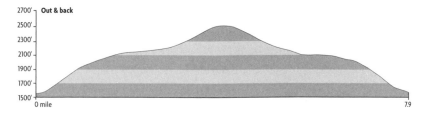

View westward from trail toward the Nine Sisters, a series of ancient volcanic plugs running from San Luis Obispo to Morro Bay

101 will be annoying for the first couple of miles until you reach the oak forest canopy and the noise becomes a distance hum.

Beyond the cattle guard and up around a wide bend and pullout, look for the brown national forest boundary marker on the right-hand side of the road. You are now entering Los Padres National Forest. Although the terrain from here is mostly exposed and the landscape relatively barren, the views continue to be stunning and the pine-covered southern slopes provide some contrast to the fascinating layers of scalloped shaled rock. This sort of exposed and frequently hot terrain requires that you carry plenty of water to keep yourself and pooch sufficiently hydrated. Apart from the far-reaching vistas, the best perk for your dog on this hike is a road-width trail for him to romp freely within view and voice control.

As you approach the top, you come to an obvious road junction with a wide eroded trail on the right heading up toward the powerlines, another dirt road going straight to some radio towers, and a gravel road to the left. Turn left onto the gravel road. The radio towers will be on your right across a pine-covered swale on the slopes of Mount Lowe. A fresh panorama of views opens eastward with a radar station at the top of Black Butte on the distant horizon. Enjoy the moments of quiet on the backside of East Cuesta Ridge as you enter a pine corridor on your way to a radio antenna building, which marks the end of the road and your destination just a short distance ahead.

Walk to the right on the outside of the fenced facility to a small, level, rocky area. This is not exactly the picnic area of your dreams, but it's as good as it gets for a snack break while you soak in more of the westward views toward San Luis Obispo and the south coast before retracing your steps down to your vehicle.

Off-trail Perks

Eagle Rock Nature Trail in El Chorro Regional Park off Highway 1 is approximately 5 miles north of San Luis Obispo and offers good views of some of the morros.

Laguna Park just off West Madonna Road at Dalidio Street in San Luis Obispo lets your dog spin out in the grassy, fenceless dog park. A clean-up bag dispenser and drinking fountain make it feel like a doggie oasis. The surrounding open space and lagoon side trails welcome dogs on leash.

Carrizo Plains National Monument, approximately 60 miles east of San Luis Obispo off Highway 58, is a 250,000-acre nature preserve managed jointly by the BLM, California Fish and Game, and the Nature Conservancy and is a unique spring and fall excursion. Contact the Goodwin Education Center, (805) 475-2131, for information on road conditions, seasonal restrictions, and dog-friendly trails.

SIERRA FOOTHILLS

The transition from the flatlands to the Sierra peaks brings undulating oak-studded grasslands sustained by snow-fed seasonal streams and rivers. Caressing spring breezes, green meadows veiled with the bright bloom of wildflowers, and a lot of water makes spring an idyllic time for hiking the foothills.

Late fall's explosion of orange and gold, crisp mornings, and warm afternoons, makes it an ideal season for hiking and midday picnics in the foothills. Summer hikes can be unpleasantly hot, so hike in the morning and stick to river or lakeside trails.

MARIPOSA

16. Merced River Trail

Round-trip: 4.78 miles, OB
Hiking time: 2 hours
Elevation range: 904–1129 feet
Difficulty: Easy, less fit okay
Season: Early spring to late fall
Pleasers and teasers: Off leash, river, solitude, spring wildflowers, convenient campground; summer temperatures can rise into the three digits
Map: USGS Bear Valley
Information: BLM Folsom Field Office, (916) 985-4474, *www.blm.gov/ca/st/en/prog/recreation/trails_intro.html*; Briceburg Visitor Center, (209) 379-9414 (usually open from the third weekend in April to Labor Day, open on weekends)

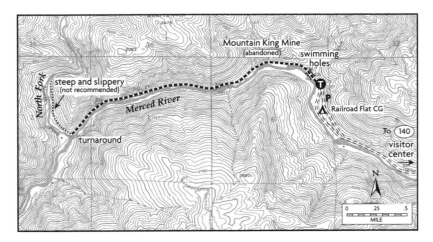

Getting there: From Merced on Highway 99, drive 37 miles east on Highway 140 to Mariposa. Continue 17.5 miles from the intersection of Highway 140 and Highway 49 North. Turn left at Bear Creek, just before Bear Creek bridge at the bottom of the long, winding descent to the Merced River canyon. The stone building on the left is the BLM Briceburg and Merced River Recreation Area information center.

Make an immediate left past the visitor center, cross the one-lane suspension bridge, and turn left toward the campgrounds. The blacktop road becomes a flat and narrow but well-maintained gravel road after the campground sign. (McCabe Flat is at 2.3 miles, Willow Placer at 3.6 miles, and Railroad Flat at 4.5 miles.) The trailhead is just beyond the westernmost campsite in the Railroad Flat campground.

If you are camping, you can walk from your campsite to the gated trailhead just beyond the campground. If you are here for the day, park along the wide shoulder area past the campground at the trailhead.

On the trail: This stretch of the Wild and Scenic Merced River Trail is within the Merced River Recreation Area under the BLM. This is a level, lightly used trail suitable for all canines and their humans.

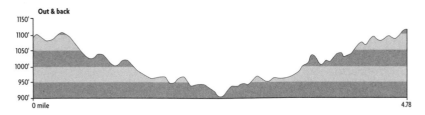

Murphy in the Merced River

From the trailhead gate, the trail is a continuation of the gravel road on which you arrived and follows the river along the old railroad right-of-way, where trains shuttled passengers from Merced east to El Portal in Yosemite National Park from 1907 to 1946. The construction of Highway 140 in the 1920s eventually replaced the trains. You come to another bridge and gate crossing Hall's Gulch, a tumbling seasonal stream with irresistible swimming holes that you will appreciate on warm days in the late spring and early summer on the return from your hike. After passing a house that overlooks the river and rusted gear from the mining heydays, the trail narrows and hugs the river as it flows unrestrained and at times furiously within the canyon rock walls.

Two miles down the trail, the north fork of the Merced River merges in from a canyon on the right. Although the trail continues for another mile up the north fork canyon to pleasant swimming holes, the precariously primitive and sometimes slippery trail is not recommended. It's best to confine your explorations to the flat area around the bend and the tamer pools below. Not to mention that on warmer days when rattlesnakes may be sunning themselves under a rock shelf along the trail, the sound of the rushing water may muffle the sound of a rattle intended to alert you and your dog. There is no room for error, panic, or surprise on these steep slopes.

At one time the hike would have taken you across the North Fork along the Merced River and all the way to Bagby Recreation Area on Highway 49, another 5 miles downstream. But landslides have obliterated parts of the trail, making the trek a thankless ordeal. Stick to the pleasurable excursion to the North Fork and back.

OAKHURST

17. Lewis Creek National Scenic Trail

Round-trip: 6.55 miles, OB
Hiking time: 3 hours
Elevation range: 3360–4291 feet
Difficulty: Easy to moderate, less fit okay
Season: Late spring to late fall
Pleasers and teasers: Off leash, creek, shade
Maps: USGS White Chief Mountain, USGS Fish Camp
Information: Sierra National Forest, Bass Lake Ranger District, (559) 877-2218, *www.fs.fed.us/r5/sierra*

Getting there: From Oakhurst at Highway 49, drive 5 miles north along Highway 41. Turn right on Cedar Valley Drive. Follow Cedar Valley Drive downhill for 1 mile to a parking area on the right of the road, just before the dip and the 25 mph sign on the right and the notice sign for the Cedar Valley subdivision on the left. If you drive over the creek and see the Cedarbrooks Drive street sign, you've gone too far. The trailhead is across the road from the parking area.

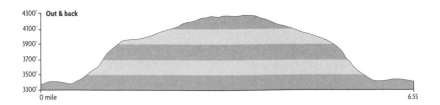

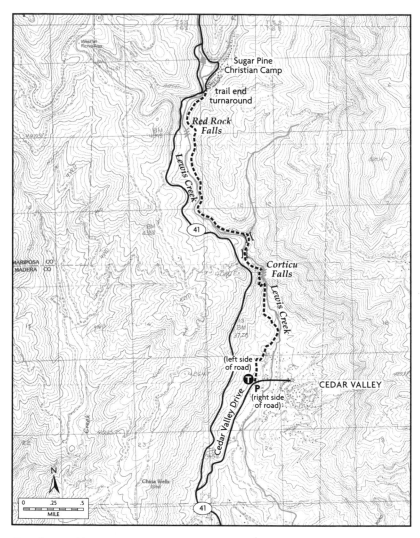

On the trail: This easily accessed, delightfully straightforward hike along shady Lewis Creek follows the historic path of the Sugar Pine lumber flume. The pine-carpeted trail stretches more than 3 miles crossing two scenic footbridges in a long, gradual uphill with a few steep spurts where the trail rises above the creek. The highlight of this hike is the journey itself rather than the destination.

The trail meets the creek within 0.25 mile and almost immediately veers left and uphill above the creek past a three-tier waterfall with doggie-perfect swimming holes. Begin climbing out of the creek bed along the

Lewis Creek

steepest stretch of the trail as you approach the midway point marked by a sign with arrows pointing in either direction for the Lewis Creek Trail. You are just below a roadside parking area for another Highway 41 trailhead to Lewis Creek Trail.

From here, the terrain will be mostly level, interrupted by gentle rises until the trail intersects abruptly and anticlimactically with the paved road into Sugar Pine Christian Camp and a few residences. Enjoy the easy stride downhill back to the trailhead. Dogs seem to find the return journey particularly invigorating as they stampede down the straightaways, tails disappearing around the bends.

WESTERN SIERRA NEVADA

The thickly forested western side of the Sierra Nevada—Spanish for "snow-covered range," and named by early explorers—with its hidden lakes and glacial streams, rises gently and gradually above the string of foothill towns rooted in gold rush history. On the doorstep of these foothill communities are a myriad of national forest trails, some brushing the backcountry boundaries of majestic Yosemite National Park and its less famous but equally sublime sister parks to the south—Kings Canyon National Park (the second oldest park; Yellowstone was the first), and Sequoia National Park (safe haven to some of the largest living trees on earth).

The northern section of the Giant Sequoia National Monument nestled between Kings Canyon and Sequoia National Park, offers the unique privilege of allowing you and your pooch to gallivant on national forest and monument trails by day, and snuggle in any of the several campgrounds within either Kings Canyon or Sequoia National Park at night.

Those willing to drive a little farther and work a little harder will find trails in the Western Sierra Nevada that provide dogs and their owners a multitude of equally stellar and sometimes more serene hiking experiences than in the national parks.

FRESNO

18. Dinkey Lakes

Round-trip: 6.86 miles, SL
Hiking time: 4 hours or overnight at Mystery Lake
Elevation range: 8606–9393 feet
Difficulty: Moderate
Season: Summer, fall
Pleasers and teasers: Off leash, lake, shade, good overnight;
  mosquitoes in summer
Map: USGS Dog Tooth Peak
Information: Sierra National Forest, High Sierra Ranger District,
  (559) 855-5360, *www.fs.fed.us/r5/sierra*

Getting there: From Fresno, drive 50 miles east on Highway 168 to
Shaver Lake. Take a right on Dinkey Creek Road. Drive 9 miles on this
paved road and turn left on Forest Road 9S09 at the sign for Dinkey
Creek trailhead. Continue on this rough road for 4.7 miles and turn right
on FR 9S10, following the sign for Dinkey Creek trailhead. These last 2
miles will be on a dirt road that frankly will seem like an improvement
over the last stretch of road. Follow this road to the end at the parking
area for the trailhead.

On the trail: This Dinkey Lakes Wilderness hike takes you past four
lakes and several meadows at the edge of the forest cradled by granite
mounds. The trail is mostly on a level to moderate grade except for the
necessary short, strenuous sprints between lakes. This jaunt is made to
order for dogs that love to scurry, splash, and be merry. Coincidentally,
according to the forest service, the area was named after a little dog, who
reportedly tussled with a grizzly in these parts in 1889.

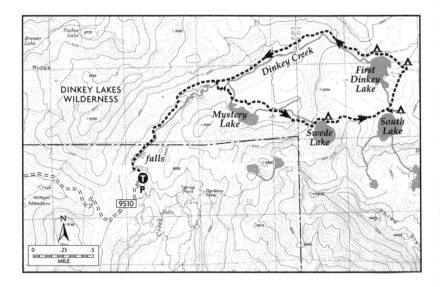

The trail begins at the end of the road and drops down to the creek's edge, the first of two creek crossings along this semi-loop. Enter Dinkey Lakes Wilderness 0.25 mile up the trail. At the sign for Mystery Lake and Dinkey Lakes, turn right toward Mystery Lake. The loop can be traveled from either direction, but hiking counterclockwise allows hikers' upward efforts to be rewarded with a lake a mile until reaching First Dinkey Lake, the last on the circuit before beginning the gradual descent to the trailhead.

The trail climbs to Mystery Lake on your right. Traverse a meadow that is equally beautiful with its veil of bright summer wildflowers as it is with the cloak of autumn gold. Continue to Swede Lake and its dramatic granite backdrop before ascending to skirt the shores of lovely South Lake on your right. The trail now begins to veer left away from South Lake and downward toward First Dinkey Lake.

You'll catch a glimpse of First Dinkey Lake almost immediately. Follow the trail toward the expansive lake's boggy outline to where it heads away from the lake before coming around to the north shore and revealing a spectacular view of the granite mounds as you look back across the lake. Follow the trail paralleling the shore as it descends westward to the intersection where you turned right to Mystery Lake earlier on. Continue down to the parking lot.

Opposite: First Dinkey Lake

19. Rancheria Falls

Round-trip: 1.66 miles, OB
Hiking time: 1 hour
Elevation range: 7576–7755 feet
Difficulty: Easy to moderate, less fit okay
Season: Spring, summer, fall
Pleasers and teasers: Off leash, bursting waterfall in spring
Maps: USGS Huntington Lake, USGS Kaiser Peak
Information: Sierra National Forest, High Sierra Ranger District, (559) 855-5360, *www.fs.fed.us/r5/sierra*

Getting there: From Fresno, drive 70 miles east on Highway 168 to Huntington Lake. Drive 1.5 miles past Sierra Summit Ski Resort and take the first paved road on your right. The sign for Rancheria Falls is turned

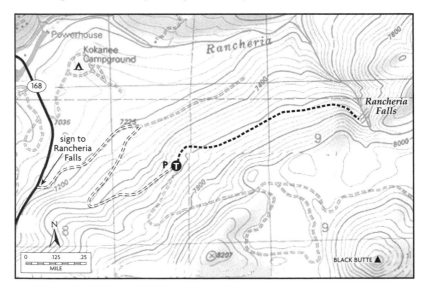

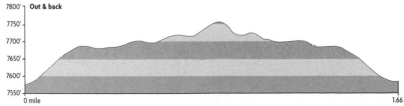

Rancheria Falls

such that you're more apt to catch it in your rearview mirror as you drive by. Drive 1.3 miles along a dirt road up to the paved parking area at the sharp curve in the road. The trailhead is just beyond the bathroom.

On the trail: What you see is what you get on this one. A short, moderate climb to a 150-foot waterfall is impressive enough for the trail to be designated as a national recreational trail.

GIANT SEQUOIA NATIONAL MONUMENT (NORTH)

magine hiking with your dog on the doorstep of spectacular Kings Canyon National Park (the second oldest national park; Yellowstone was the first), and precious Sequoia National Park (safe haven to some of the largest living trees on earth). That's the incredible privilege that comes with hiking in Giant Sequoia National Monument. You and pooch can snuggle in any of the several campgrounds within the two national parks at night and spend your days gallivanting on the trails of the national forest and monument lands nestled between the two parks.

20. Boole Tree Loop

Round-trip: 2.1 miles, L
Hiking time: 1.5 hours
Elevation range: 6270–6845 feet
Difficulty: Easy, less fit okay
Season: Spring, summer, fall
Pleasers and teasers: Off leash, shade
Map: USGS Hume
Information: Sequoia National Forest, Hume Lake Ranger District, (559) 338-2251, *www.fs.fed.us/r5/sequoia*

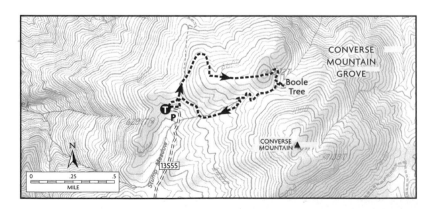

Getting there: From Fresno, drive 55 miles east on Highway 180 to the Big Stump Entrance of Kings Canyon National Park. Drive 1.5 miles and turn left into the park and Grant Grove Village. Drive 4 miles past Grant Grove and make a left turn at Forest Road 13S55 and the Boole Tree sign. Follow the dirt road for 2.5 miles to the trailhead parking. You'll traverse a ghostly meadow of scattered Sequoia stumps—a graveyard that serves as a reminder of an era when these majestic living giants were mowed down before awareness gave life to places like Sequoia National Park.

The majestic Boole Tree

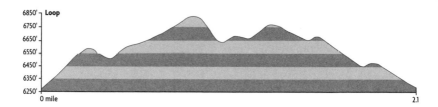

On the trail: The bonus on this loop is the stunning views of Kings Canyon leading to the largest of the Sequoia trees in a national forest. Ironically, the 269-foot-tall Boole Tree was named after the superintendent of the lumber company who supervised the cutting of the grove, except for this one tree.

The trail begins to the left with a moderate incline to an open ridge that reveals the magnificent grandeur of the Sierra Nevada and the Kings River canyon. Follow the trail as it levels and gradually descends into the forest. If you look over the forest canopy, you will spot the Boole Tree rising thick and tall above all others. Take the left spur trail down to the Boole Tree for a closer look at this stately, solitary sentinel before retracing your steps back to the main trail to complete your loop. While this towering wonder of the natural world is sure to awe and humble you, it's the forest floor's rich, musty carpet beneath his paws and nose that will impress Fido most.

Off-trail Perks

If you're going to be in Giant Sequoia National Monument (North), the 2.5-mile loop around Hume Lake Dam is a level, easy, and pleasant interpretive stroll for dogs of all ages and an interesting lumber history and ecology lesson for you.

From Grant Grove, drive 12 miles and take the Hume Lake turnoff on the right. Drive 3.5 miles and follow the signs to Hume Lake. Bear left at the sign for Hume Lake campground and park by the lake. Walk down to the lakeshore and begin your walk along the path in either direction. At the far end of the lake, the path is briefly interrupted by the private Christian camp (the market and gift shop are open to the public). Just stay along the lakeshore until you reconnect to the nature trail. The beach at Sandy Point is off-limits to dogs, but the stream above the bridge isn't. Follow the trail around the lake to the second bridge at the far end of the lake to loop back to your starting point.

21. Chicago Stump Trail

Round-trip: 0.55 mile, SL
Hiking time: 20 minutes
Elevation range: 6585–6693 feet
Difficulty: Easy, less fit okay
Season: Spring, summer, fall
Pleasers and teasers: Off leash, shade
Map: USGS Hume
Information: Sequoia National Forest, Hume Lake Ranger District, (559) 338-2251, *www.fs.fed.us/r5/sequoia*

Getting there: From Fresno, drive 55 miles east on Highway 180 to the Big Stump Entrance of Kings Canyon National Park. Drive 1.5 miles and turn left into the park and Grant Grove Village. Drive 3 miles past Grant Grove and turn left onto Forest Road 13S03. There is no sign on the main

A hiker checks out the Chicago Stump

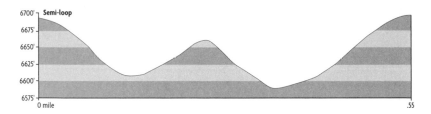

road for Chicago Stump, but you
will recognize the turnoff by the
interpretive stone plaque on the
left-hand side of the road. Follow
the dirt road for 1.8 miles toward
Chicago Stump. Make a right on
FR 13S66 and drive 0.1 mile. Park
your vehicle on the right side of
the road in a turnout just past the

Chicago Stump road sign. The trailhead is about 100 yards farther down
the road on the right. This stretch of dirt road leading to the trailhead
can be seriously eroded at times, so it's best to park and walk the 100
yards to the signed trailhead.

On the trail: The short hike to Chicago Stump follows a pleasantly wide
loop trail past a meadow on your left before arriving at the gargantuan
stump. The 3200-year-old tree was cut down, transported to, and reas-
sembled at the Chicago World's Fair in 1878 to impress the crowds who
remained convinced such a tree could not exist.

22. Weaver Lake

Round-trip: 6.65 miles, OB
Hiking time: 4 hours
Elevation range: 7585–8733 feet
Difficulty: Moderate
Season: Late spring, summer, fall
Pleasers and teasers: Off leash, lake, shade; mosquitoes in summer
Map: USGS Muir Grove
Information: Sequoia National Forest, Hume Lake Ranger District,
    (559) 338-2251, *www.fs.fed.us/r5/sequoia*

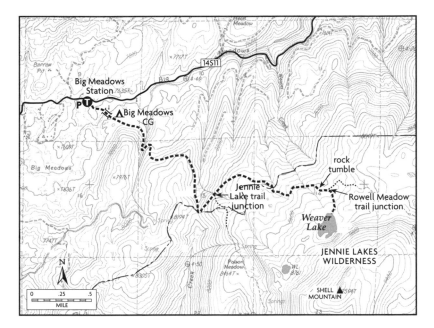

Getting there: From Fresno drive 55 miles east on Highway 180 to the Big Stump Entrance of Kings Canyon National Park. Make a right onto Generals Highway toward Sequoia National Park. Drive 7 miles along Generals Highway and turn left onto Forest Road 14S11 at the Big Meadows/Horse Corral sign. Drive 4 miles along this paved forest road, following signs for the Big Meadows trailhead. Pass the guard station on your left and a pay phone off the road on your right. The trailhead parking lot is just ahead on the right and before the Big Meadows campground. Park at the far end of the upper parking lot; the hike begins in the northeast corner of the parking lot.

There is a large map board next to the bathroom by the lower parking lot, but don't expect it to be much help. The trailhead is unmarked and obscure but is easily located if you scan for the row of rocks that have been laid down to guide you along this initial stretch of the trail.

Standing at the northeast corner of the parking lot, look down toward the lower parking area and toward the road you came in on. With the bathroom on your right, the row of rocks should be visible on your left, downslope from the parking area.

On the trail: Watch for the stream and a footbridge within a few hundred yards of the parking area. Cross the bridge and look ahead for the wooden trail marker with an arrow pointing left. All trail-locating anxieties now behind you, you and pooch can get on with the business of having fun. If you've hiked several of the other Sierra trails in this book, this one won't be the most memorable. But it has the unique distinction of being the most easily accessible lake in the Jennie Lakes Wilderness, not to mention how close pooch will get to hiking in Sequoia National Park on this trail.

On the trail, keep an eye out for the occasional wood sign with arrows directing you along the way. The trail climbs up a canyon with a stream on the right. Another trail sign directs you left and across the stream, where the trail veers uphill and away from the stream approaching a

Weaver Lake

rise with open vistas northward of the Sierra. The trail slopes down into a forested patch and then up, leading to another creek crossing at a trail junction—Jennie Lake to the right and Weaver Lake straight ahead. Cross the creek and hike 0.75 mile to the boundary of the Jennie Lakes Wilderness. At 3 miles, the trail passes through a rock tumble before a junction for Rowell Meadow. Stay on the Weaver Lake Trail. Just short of the lake, the trail seems to disappear into the loose rocks from blink to blink. Focus on the granite shelf known as Shell Mountain, peering through the trees ahead, and you will pick up the trail leading to the lake's edge, which beckons pooches and hikers to sit and enjoy the end of the trail. Have a snack while soaking in the muted beauty of Weaver Lake.

Off-trail Perks

The Buck Rock Fire Tower is worth a side trip. Follow directions in Hike 22 to Forest Road 14S11 at Big Meadows/Horse Corral off Highway 180/ Generals Highway. Turn left and drive 2.5 miles to the Buck Rock Fire Tower and campground sign. At the sign, turn left onto the dirt road and drive 2.5 miles. Drive through Buck Rock campground, and at the fork in the road, bear right toward the fire tower marker. You'll spot a few campsites along the way up to the parking area below the fire tower. Park where indicated and take the 0.25-mile round-trip hike to this amazing perch. If the tower keeper is home, you'll get a rare opportunity for a tour of these vanishing sentinels now on the National Historic Lookout Registry.

OAKHURST

23. Chiquito Pass

Round-trip: 5.29 miles, OB
Hiking time: 3–3.5 hours
Elevation range: 7246–8064 feet
Difficulty: Easy to moderate
Season: Late spring, summer, fall
Pleasers and teasers: Off leash, lake, shade; mosquitoes in summer
Map: USGS Sing Peak
Information: Sierra National Forest, Bass Lake Ranger District,
(559) 877-2218, *www.fs.fed.us/r5/sierra*

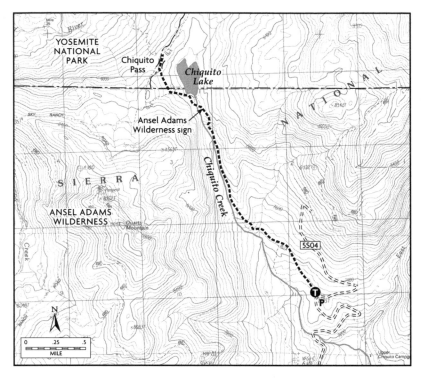

Getting there: From Oakhurst at the intersection of Highways 49 and 41, drive 3.4 miles north along Highway 41 and take the Bass Lake/Road 222 exit. Drive 5.7 miles along Road 222, which becomes Road 274. Take a left off Road 274 onto Beasore Road. You will see a sign for Chilkoot Campground, Beasore Meadow, and Clover Meadow. Follow winding Beasore Road for 20.2 miles and turn left at the Chiquito Pass trailhead sign and Forest Road 5S04. Follow the dirt road for 2.5 miles to the trailhead parking area. The trailhead is across the road from the parking area.

On the trail: Although the hike to Chiquito Pass doesn't boast dramatic scenery, it's a pleasant, forested hike, with a moderate incline, into the

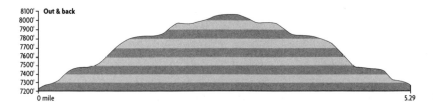

Alex prepares to tap a frozen stream with his paw.

Ansel Adams Wilderness. The first highlight of the hike is the wide-open meadow surrounding Chiquito Lake just short of the pass; the second is the location of the pass itself—right smack on the boundary of Yosemite National Park. There's something exciting about hiking to the boundary of a national park with your dog and a naughty pleasure in letting your dog set a paw, even for just a moment, on the forbidden land.

The trail climbs along gentle terrain most of the way, crossing two streams before arriving at Chiquito Lake 2 miles up the trail. The last, short, abrupt ascent to the lake begins just past the Ansel Adams Wilderness sign. The wide-open plateau at Chiquito Lake, which resembles a wetland more than a lake by late fall, is a pleasant contrast to the shady forested surroundings. Follow the level trail along the left side of the lake and finally up the last moderate incline to Chiquito Pass and the Yosemite

National Park boundary, identified by a sign and a wire fenceline. Here you'll find many granite boulders beckoning you and pooch to stop for a rest and a snack while soaking in the peaceful vibes of the wilderness.

Off-trail Perks

Consider spending an extra day around Oakhurst to drive the Sierra Vista National Scenic Byway loop. Follow the driving directions in Hike 23 from Oakhurst to Beasore Road. The scenic byway crests around 7000 feet in Sierra National Forest and passes several points of historical and geological interest, campgrounds, and windows of High Sierra views before dropping back down to North Fork. For a map, contact the Sierra Vista National Scenic Byway Association in North Fork, (559) 877-7779, www.fs.fed.us/r5/sierra.

EASTERN SIERRA NEVADA

J ust over the crest of the Sierra Nevada lies a scenic, dog-friendly paradise, where snowcapped granite peaks rise defiantly and dramatically above a high-desert wasteland of cinder cones and tumbleweeds that sweep eastward toward the Nevada border on the edge of the Great Basin.

One moment you are peering at a postcard, and the next you are in the postcard. It is easy to be seduced by this expansive landscape, where the dance of light and shadow has enchanted and mesmerized artists for decades. With every step, this spellbinding kingdom borne of wind, water, and fire reveals ecosystems teeming with life nourished by the ribbons of melting snow that drape the precipitous rocky sentinels. The water wars of decades past altered the destinies of the Owens Valley and the Eastern Sierra. As an ironic result, the diverted waters grew tract housing, malls, and orchards in Los Angeles, leaving thousands of acres of national forest along Highway 395 for outdoor enthusiasts and their dogs to enjoy. The scenery is superb; the choice of hikes dazzling.

In the summer, the most direct route to the Eastern Sierra from the west is through the fee entrance of Yosemite National Park over Tioga Pass Road (Highway 120).

=MITE—TIOGA PASS

24. Nunatak Nature Trail

Round-trip: 0.46 mile, L
Hiking time: 30 minutes
Elevation range: 9600–9668 feet
Difficulty: Easy, less fit okay
Season: Late spring, summer, fall. Access depends on the Tioga Pass Road closure schedule, which is directly linked to snow conditions. Tioga Pass is the highest of the Sierra passes for vehicles, the first to close in fall, and the last to open in spring.
Pleasers and teasers: Off leash, ponds, shade, no fleas, views; mosquitoes can be brutal in summer
Maps: USGS Mount Dana, USGS Tioga Pass
Information: Inyo National Forest, Lee Vining Ranger District, (760) 873-2408, summer only; call Mammoth Lakes Ranger District, (760) 924-5500, in the winter months; *www.fs.fed.us/r5/inyo*

Getting there: From the town of Mammoth Lakes, drive 25 miles north on Highway 395 to the Tioga Road/Highway 120/Yosemite National Park turnoff. Turn left onto Highway 120 and drive 10 miles west to the trailhead and parking area on the right just above Tioga Pass Resort cabins.

On the trail: This very short but delightful trail is a great warm-up and microcosm of the beauty and pleasures that lie ahead if you are on your way to the Eastern Sierra. It is also a fitting and final opportunity for Fido to enjoy a last saunter and breath of dog-friendly nature if you are leaving the east side and journeying through divinely beautiful but not so dog-compatible Yosemite National Park.

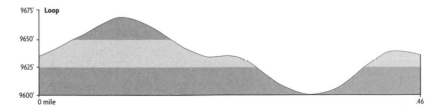

The author with Alex and Moses on Nunatak Nature Trail

The first 250 feet of the trail is paved for wheelchair access, and the remaining pathway is dirt, meandering through the trees and etching the shores of a few small ponds. These ponds are known as tarns, legacy of the retreating glaciers several thousand years ago. A nunatak is a hill or mountain protruding above the sea of ice that surrounds it. As young and old pooches enjoy this macro-wilderness experience, you can brush up on the natural history and geology of the High Sierra by reading the interpretive signs along the way. There is a picnic table at the beginning of the trail and a bench partway around, both conducive to snacking and pondering.

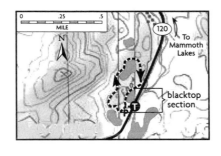

Although you can have your dog off leash, be aware that the trail skirts Highway 120 back to the parking area, and it's safest to put your dog on leash if he's the impulsive, exuberant type.

25. Glacier Canyon

Round-trip: 4.39 miles, OB
Hiking time: 3.5–4 hours
Elevation range: 9664–11,152 feet
Difficulty: Moderate to strenuous, less-fit route option
Season: Summer, fall
Pleasers and teasers: Off leash, creek, lake, boulders, no fleas; mosquitoes in summer
Maps: USGS Mount Dana, USGS Tioga Pass
Information: Inyo National Forest, Lee Vining Ranger District, (760) 873-2408, summer only; call Mammoth Lakes Ranger District, (760) 924-5500, in the winter months; *www.fs.fed.us/r5/inyo*

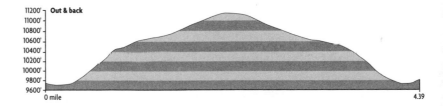

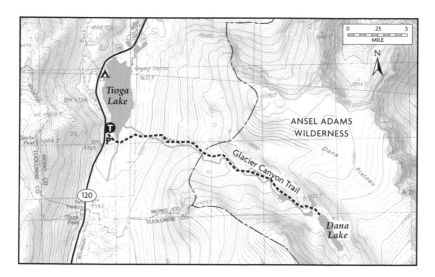

Getting there: From the town of Mammoth Lakes, drive 25 miles north on Highway 395 to the Tioga Road/Highway 120/Yosemite National Park turnoff. Turn left onto Highway 120 and drive 11 miles west to the Tioga Lake parking lot at the Tioga overlook sign on your left at the west end of the lake.

On the trail: Somehow this is the trail that maps forgot. Glacier Canyon's streams, meadows, trees, picnic spots, and Kodak moments may be one of the Yosemite area's best-kept secrets from dogs and their owners.

The trail climbs moderately, tracing the creek in mostly open terrain with expansive high-country views every step and almost every direction of the way up to a green valleylike plateau below the stark and barren glacial tarns known as Dana Lakes.

The unmarked but obvious trail from the roadside parking lot to the western shoreline of Tioga Lake descends behind the restrooms. Follow the trail to the water's edge, walking counterclockwise around the west end of the lake. The trail splits as you approach the south shore. Take the right spur trail up the gentle rise, and you will see the wooden trail sign for Dana Lakes and Glacier Canyon.

Glacier Canyon Trail passes through a tightly growing pine grove and then opens up to a rockier stretch, with the stream initially flowing on your left until you cross it just a short way ahead. The stream will remain on your right the rest of the way. Enter the Ansel Adams Wilderness at the first plateau as the sign indicates. The trail veers right and upslope along a more obscure trail lined with "ducks" or cairns (stacked rocks) from time to time. The trail levels out one final time atop the last green plateau, which is fed by the glacial ribbons from Dana Lakes at the far end of the valley. At this point, the lakes are still hidden by a large moraine 0.5 mile ahead.

The trail hugs a large granite table on the left and continues along the east end of the meadow. These granite slabs are perfect for picnicking and soaking in the soaring views of the surrounding peaks; the meadow is dog-romping heaven.

Beyond this point, the trail to Dana Lakes is at times barely discernable and crosses some talus slopes and hand-over-hand scrambles. The landscape surrounding the stark glacial tarns can only be described as barren. Frankly, at the risk of committing High Sierra blasphemy, this meadow and its superlative setting is a far more rewarding destination than Dana Lakes.

The downhill return trip is easy enough that you can take your eyes off your feet to enjoy the bird's-eye view of this majestic realm.

Less-fit route option: Hike around Tioga Lake.

Dana Lake at end of Glacier Canyon Trail

26. Gardisky Lake

Round-trip: 1.6 miles, OB
Hiking time: 2 hours
Difficulty: Strenuous
Elevation range: 9752–10,487 feet
Season: Summer, fall
Pleasers and teasers: Off leash, lake, no fleas, wildflowers, solitude, views; mosquitoes in summer
Map: USGS Tioga Pass
Information: Inyo National Forest, Lee Vining Ranger District, (760) 873-2408, summer only; call Mammoth Lakes Ranger District, (760) 924-5500, in the winter months; *www.fs.fed.us/r5/inyo*

Getting there: From the town of Mammoth Lakes, drive 25 miles north on Highway 395 to the Tioga Road/Highway 120/Yosemite National Park turnoff. Turn left onto Highway 120 and drive 9.5 miles west to the Saddlebag Lake exit on the right. Follow the signs for Saddlebag Lake campground, and go 1.1 miles along the gravel road to the Gardisky Lake parking lot on the left. The trailhead is just across the road on the right.

On the trail: This short, demanding cardio sprint is an incredibly rewarding hike but best appreciated after a couple of days of acclimatization. Even if you feel an adrenaline spike coming on because it's less than a mile, it's not fair or safe to crank your dog from sofa or backyard mode straight into Gardisky gear.

Start this hike in the morning when the trail is still in the shade of pines and cool of spring melt-fed grasses. The trail climbs relentlessly, tempered only by the occasional switchback. Watch your footing on the slippery rock as you cross the stream that steps down the face of the slope. From this point up, the stream remains within sight, sound, or

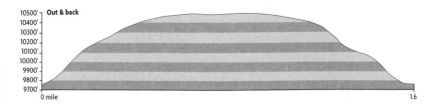

The pristine beauty of Gardisky Lake

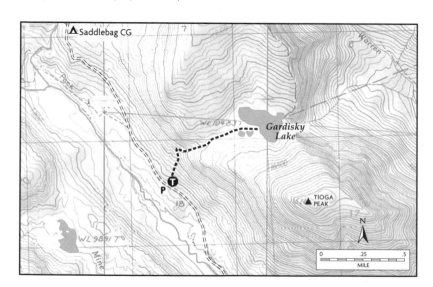

touch, and the firm dirt trail transitions to a mix of rock, dirt, and scree as you and pooch boogie on up.

One last hamstring stretch over some high, flat stepping-stones, and the open, green plateau is your gateway to Gardisky Lake. Follow the trail along the narrowing stream that feeds this awesome alpine meadow. Gardisky Lake is set back, its shallow waters brimming to the naturally manicured green edge with two idyllic ponds in the foreground and majestic views of Tioga Peak behind you. This virginal landscape inspires higher levels of respect and appreciation for nature's gifts. Savor the moment before retracing your steps along the streamside meadow footpath and carefully down the steep and potentially slippery trail to your vehicle.

27. Saddlebag Lake

Round-trip: 4.22 miles, L
Hiking time: 3.5 hours
Elevation range: 10,070–10,275 feet
Difficulty: Easy, less fit okay
Season: Summer, fall
Pleasers and teasers: Off leash, lake, no fleas, views; talus stretch of
    trail abrasive on paws, mosquitoes in summer
Map: USGS Tioga Pass
Information: Inyo National Forest, Lee Vining Ranger District,
    (760) 873-2408, summer only; call Mammoth Lakes Ranger District, (760) 924-5500, in the winter months; *www.fs.fed.us/r5/inyo*

Getting there: From the town of Mammoth Lakes, drive 25 miles north on Highway 395 to the Tioga Road/Highway 120/Yosemite National Park turnoff. Turn left and drive 9.5 miles west to the Saddlebag Lake turnoff on the right. Drive 2 miles to Saddlebag Resort. Continue to the end of

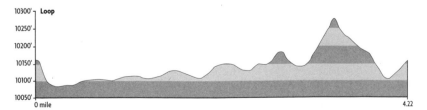

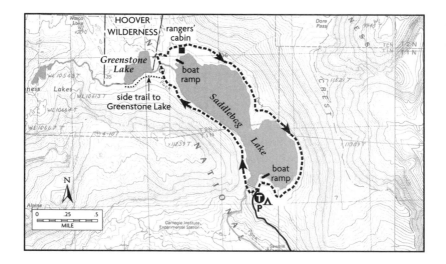

the road and park in the lot in front of the resort. The trailhead parking lot on the right is for backpackers.

On the trail: At first glance, Saddlebag Resort and the human imprint of the dam at the south end are disappointing, and the easy loop hike around this long body of water seems like a cop-out. Don't be fooled. This hike will unveil some idyllic surprises along the way.

The official trailhead for the Saddlebag loop is to the right of the parking lot and would have you doing the loop counterclockwise. But in the spirit of keeping the best for last, do this hike clockwise. You will get the rough talus (shale rock with sharp edges) stretch of trail on the west side over at the start. The views and trail surface along the east side will seem more rewarding on the return.

From the parking lot, walk back down the road toward the lower side of the dam behind the green forest service utility building. Follow the trail down and below the dam to the locked gate. The dam overflow goes through an underground pipe, so walking across to the other side from this low point is a nonissue. Climb up the rise to the west shore along the rocky four-wheel-drive access and look for the less-official trailhead sign at the edge of the lake.

Begin your hike above the lake and watch your footing along the talus slope path for the first third of the way. As you approach the north shore, you'll be met by green meadows with wildflower patches in bursts of crimson and violet during the summer months and the nourishing

Hikers along the Saddlebag loop

Moses takes in the view at Saddlebag Lake.

stands of pine. Take the fork to the left for a short but worthwhile jaunt to Greenstone Lake, a shallow lake of exquisite beauty fed by multiple veins of snowmelt streams in the heart of what could be Scottish Highland moors. The sculpted peaks and ridges that ring this alpine setting are truly nature's masterpiece. Follow the trail across a log footbridge, and make your way along the pond and back toward Saddlebag Lake's main trail.

As you reach the north end of the lake, the rangers' summer cabin sits between the lake and the Hoover Wilderness in idyllic simplicity. Continue your loop back to the parking lot along the east shore of the lake, where there are several convenient lake accesses for pooch to wet his paws.

Less-fit route option: Cut the hike in half by cruising across the lake on the water taxi (purchase tickets at the Saddlebag Resort store) and hike back along the eastern shore.

Off-trail Perks

The Mono Basin National Forest Scenic Visitor Center, 0.25 mile north of Lee Vining, is a must do. The center has a wealth of information and fascinating exhibits about the history and ecology of this ancient lake (more than 700,000 years old and three times saltier than the ocean). Dogs are not allowed in the visitor center, but you and pooch can get a close-up look at the surreal tufas (limestone towers created by underwater springs) along the South Tufa Trail on the southern shore of Mono Lake. The trailhead is off Highway 120 East. Mono Basin National Forest Scenic Visitor Center, (760) 647-3044, www.monolake.org .

JUNE LAKE

28. Fern Lake ✓

Round-trip: 3.38 miles, OB
Hiking time: 2.5–3 hours
Elevation range: 7303–8885 feet
Difficulty: Strenuous; less-fit option for 1.1 mile turnaround
Season: Summer, fall
Pleasers and teasers: Off leash, lake, shade, no fleas, views; mosquitoes in summer
Map: USGS Mammoth Mountain
Information: Inyo National Forest, Lee Vining Ranger District, (760) 873-2408, summer only; call Mammoth Lakes Ranger District, (760) 924-5500, in the winter months; www.fs.fed.us/r5/inyo

Getting there: From the town of Mammoth Lakes, drive 15 miles north on Highway 395 to the southern entrance of the June Lake Loop (State Route 158) turnoff and turn left. Drive 5 miles, and then pay close attention for the small trailhead sign on the left side of the road at 5.2 miles. Turn left and drive 0.1 mile to the dirt parking area.

On the trail: This hike is relentless in its ascent but short enough and definitely rewarding enough to be worth the workout. You'll be awed by the views and pooch will love the shallow, cool wading waters of Fern

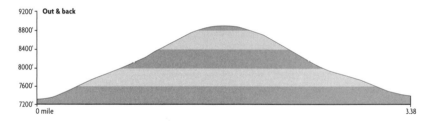

Lake, not to mention the most perfect picnic rock on the breezy edge of the lake.

Before you step onto the narrow, sandy trail squeezed between two boulders, point pooch to the stream on the left of the parking area for a prehike plunge. Start on the somewhat obscure trail that leads to a map board and the more obvious trail ahead. The trail climbs consistently over the first mile out of the aspen and pines to more exposed slopes where the views gradually unfold into a bowl-like panorama of peaks cradling Silver Lake, Gull Lake, and June Lake below. You'll reach a trail intersection at 1.1 miles, just below where Fern Creek tumbles down and across the trail ahead. At this point, if you feel short on time or energy, you have the option of taking a few steps past the intersection to the creek crossing, a pleasant destination for many hikers with children and dogs. Just retrace your steps down at your leisure.

If you and your dog are still feeling spirited by the time you reach the intersection, turn right and push on to Fern Lake. As if to reward your efforts and distract you from your panting, this steeper, exposed section

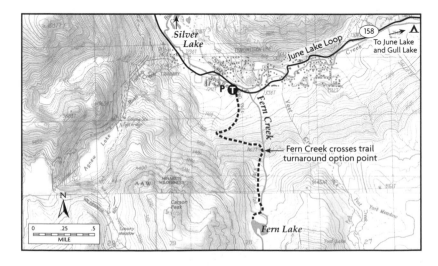

of the trail also reveals some very dramatic views of Gull Lake and June
Lake, with its dazzling aqua ribbon rimming the beach at the far end.

The creek remains in view for a while as the trail levels into the forest
before the last sharp climb into the bowl that cradles Fern Lake.

You may see ducks paddle to the shore to greet the hikers, oblivious
to the dogs that can't believe their luck at finding floating, squeaky
toys in the forest. Do not feed these wild animals, and put your dog on
leash until you find a duck-free swimming area. After a sufficient dose
of mountain bliss, retrace your steps to the parking area.

Alex and Moses playing in Fern Lake

29. Yost Lake

Round-trip: 4.8 miles, OB
Hiking time: 3–3.5 hours
Elevation range: 7303–9093 feet
Difficulty: Moderate
Season: Summer, fall
Pleasers and teasers: Off leash, lake, shade, no fleas, views; mosquitoes in summer
Map: USGS Mammoth Mountain
Information: Inyo National Forest, Lee Vining Ranger District, (760) 873-2408, summer only; call Mammoth Lakes Ranger District, (760) 924-5500, in the winter months; *www.fs.fed.us/r5/inyo*

Getting there: From the town of Mammoth Lakes, drive 15 miles north on Highway 395 to the southern entrance of the June Lake Loop turnoff and turn left. Drive 5 miles, and then pay close attention for the small trailhead sign on the left side of the road at 5.2 miles. Turn left and drive 0.1 mile to the dirt parking area.

On the trail: In the Sierra, if there's a view, a stream, or a lake, it's worth the effort. The trail to Yost Lake has all three.

Start at the trailhead for Hike 28, Fern Lake, and when you reach the intersection for Fern Lake to the right at 1.1 miles and Yost Lake straight ahead, continue straight. Cross the refreshing creek on the rocks if water levels permit or cross the narrow log footbridge hovering a few feet above the plunging creek. It's at a crossing like this one where you will understand why a harness—as opposed to a collar of any type—on your dog is the safest hiking attire.

Once over the adrenaline rush of the creek crossing, continue up the slopeside trail as it climbs gradually but steadily, alternating between

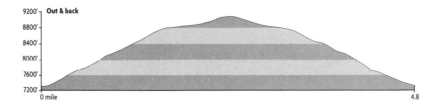

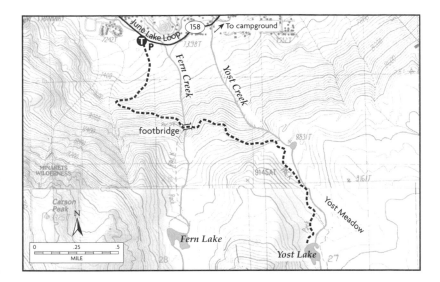

Watch your dog closely on the log footbridge at Yost Creek.

ed view sheds and cool, shaded glens. Halfway along the hike, the levels as it passes through a pine forest with Yost Creek in sight on the left. You will come across a sign for Yost Lake straight ahead, Yost Meadow to the left, and Highway 158 pointing in the direction you came from. Continue straight ahead to Yost Lake as the trail rises mildly toward the foot of a remarkable jagged escarpment and as Yost Lake comes into view a few yards ahead. There is more vegetation along the shoreline than at Fern Lake (Hike 28), but your dog will find more than one suitable access for a splash or a paddle.

The return trip is simple, but pay attention to the sign at the intersection for Yost Meadow to the right, making sure you bear left and retrace your steps down the trail to Highway 158 where your vehicle is parked.

MAMMOTH LAKES

30. Sherwin Lakes ✓

Round-trip: 4.91 miles, OB
Hiking time: 3–3.5 hours
Difficulty: Moderate
Elevation range: 7823–8702 feet
Season: Summer, fall
Pleasers and teasers: Off leash, lake, shade, no fleas, views, wildflowers, golden aspens in fall; mosquitoes in summer
Map: USGS Bloody Mountain
Information: Inyo National Forest, Mammoth Ranger District, (760) 924-5500, *www.fs.fed.us/r5/inyo, www.visitmammoth.com*

Getting there: From the town of Mammoth Lakes, drive 2.5 miles east on Highway 203 to Highway 395. Drive 1 mile south on Highway 395 and turn right onto Sherwin Creek Road. Drive 4 miles along the maintained gravel road to the Sherwin Lakes trailhead turnoff on your left. Drive 0.25 mile along this gravel spur to the trailhead parking lot.

On the trail: Sherwin Lakes consist of five lakes nestled in the Sherwin Range on the east edge of the town of Mammoth Lakes. Except for

crossing Sherwin Creek close to the start of the trail, the uphill hike is very dry until you reach the lakes. Make sure you carry enough water for you and your dog.

The loose dirt trail begins through mostly high-desert sagebrush, which quickly transitions to pine trees where you cross Sherwin Creek on a wooden footbridge. The trail starts to climb gradually, approaching an exposed slope of manzanita. About 0.75 mile into the hike, the trail switchbacks through a weather-ravaged gully of fallen trees and past a rockfall rising above the boulder-lined trail before reaching the pine plateau. The views open to the stretches of forest and meadows below. The loose dirt eventually turns to calf-toning soft sand, which may add to your exertion factor but will make pooch feel light on his toes. After a few more bends in the trail, you'll get a peek of peaks through the trees. The last couple of switchbacks will be tighter until the trail straightens, widens, and levels out just before rolling downward into the pine basin where you will hear the sound of nearby water and catch a surprising glimpse of a Matterhorn-like peak between the trees.

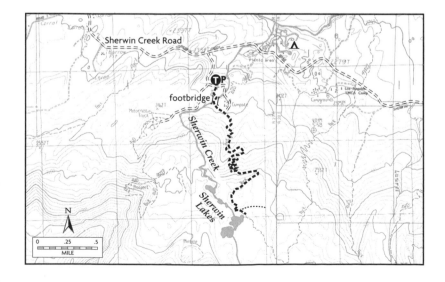

The serene setting of Sherwin Lake

The trail serpentines, putting the Matterhorn peak ahead and slightly to your right as the first of the Sherwin Lakes comes into view also on your right. Don't let your pooch pass up this opportunity for a splash.

Continue along a narrow, large boulder-lined pathway, which makes dogs feel like they're on a luge racing down a chute. You'll catch another glimpse of a Sherwin lake as the trail leans away from the water. Follow the trail to the Y and a sign nailed to a tree with one arrow pointing right for Sherwin Lakes and another pointing left for Valentine Lake.

Go right toward Sherwin Lakes, where the trail rises slightly with one lake to your right and the other above to your left. The trail enters a denser forest for a few yards and emerges at the rushing stream where it pours from the upper lake into the lower lake. You can easily reach the upper lake's shore through the overgrown foliage, but it's the lower, larger lake just a few steps below that is the prize. You can see it from this side of the stream, and depending on the winter's snowpack, by midsummer you can usually cross the stream with minimal acrobatic experience along the fallen limb footbridge. Retrace your steps down the trail back to your vehicle.

31. Valentine Lake

Round-trip: 9.83 miles, OB
Hiking time: 5.5–6.5 hours
Elevation range: 7823–9849 feet
Difficulty: Moderate to strenuous
Season: Summer, fall
Pleasers and teasers: Off leash, lake, shade, no fleas, views; mosqui-
toes in summer
Map: USGS Bloody Mountain
Information: Inyo National Forest, Mammoth Ranger District,
(760) 924-5500, *www.fs.fed.us/r5/inyo*

Getting there: From the town of Mammoth Lakes, drive 2.5 miles east
on Highway 203 to Highway 395. Drive 1 mile south on Highway 395 and
take a right onto Sherwin Creek Road. Drive 4 miles along the maintained
gravel road to the Sherwin Lakes trailhead turnoff on your left. Drive 0.25
mile along this gravel spur to the trailhead parking lot.

On the trail: You and pooch will enjoy the moderate jaunt past stands
of striking Sierra junipers on your way to an idyllic glacial lake at the base
of a granite palisade. There are two trailhead possibilities for Valentine
Lake, as well as a loop option. This hike describes the out-and-back route
from the Sherwin Lakes trailhead, Hike 30, for two reasons: The terrain
itself is almost identical on both routes, but the loop adds almost 2 extra
unrewarding, dry, dusty miles along Sherwin Creek Road.

Begin at the Sherwin Lakes trailhead and follow the route described
in Hike 30 until you reach the Y. Take time to go right to Sherwin Lakes
for a refreshing stop before retracing those few steps back to the Y and
heading left up the trail to Valentine Lake.

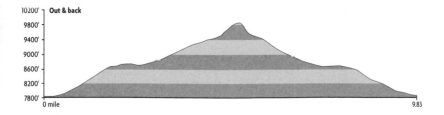

On the way to Valentine Lake

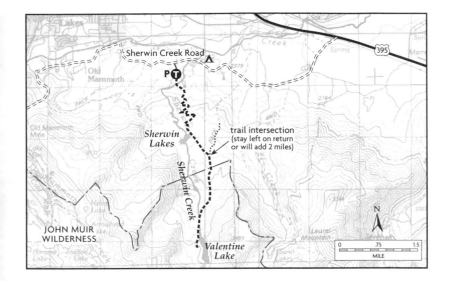

The route to Valentine Lake promises a medley of natural beauty beginning with a gradual, moderate climb of 2.5 miles, culminating with a strenuous 0.5-mile stretch of switchbacks to climb atop this glacial cul-de-sac.

About 0.25 mile after your left turn onto the Valentine Lake Trail from the Y, the trail and soil in the meadow becomes sandier and dotted with midsummer lupine and the Sierra junipers that are unique to this area. Their distinctive and massive reddish trunks, some ten feet in diameter with bark as soft as straw, are a treat to admire and caress.

Beyond this stand of junipers, the trail dips where a seasonal stream flows from the right. The trail switchbacks up for a short, steady climb to yet another welcome, flat meadow with a display of Sierra junipers. Ahead on the right, a sign for Valentine Lake is nailed to a tree, and the terrain transitions from sand to rock and root steps. You soon come to a trail intersection with a signpost indicating that the way to Sherwin Lakes is to the right (where you are coming from) and Valentine Lake is straight ahead.

Make a mental note of this intersection for the return. On your return, be sure to turn left toward Sherwin Lakes. If you proceed straight and miss the left turn, you will be committed to looping back, which adds the extra 2 miles along Sherwin Creek Road mentioned earlier.

After you pass the sign marking the boundary of and enter the John Muir Wilderness, the trail alternates between level stretches and climbing.

You will hear the intermittent sound of the stream before entering a willowy, moist, and somewhat-overgrown domain. It's a good idea to put pooch on leash and make your presence known with loud chat or singing whenever you hike through thickly vegetated patches where you might surprise a munching bear.

The trail soon emerges onto rockier terrain on the edge of the pine-needle and pinecone carpet pathway ahead, passing a nameless marshy lake to the right. Notice the granite palisade on your right, beyond the cascading waters announcing Valentine Lake above. You're on the final 0.5-mile stretch of the push-and-pull game with the roaring tumble of water. Valentine Lake and the gray craggy crest that cradles its pristine shores and guards its solitude is almost in sight.

Once you reach the mouth of the cascading waters pouring out of Valentine Lake—if the seasonal flow is tempered enough—it is fairly easy for you and pooch to negotiate a crossing for a scramble to the top in search of the perfect picnic perch, with enough breeze to keep the summer mosquitoes at bay.

Retrace your steps back to your vehicle while keeping an eye out for that strategic intersection and remembering to turn left at the sign for Sherwin Lakes.

Peaceful and pristine Valentine Lake

32. Laurel Lakes

Round-trip: 10.05 miles, OB
Hiking time: 6.5–8 hours or overnight at creekside campsite
Difficulty: Strenuous
Elevation range: 7375–10,095 feet
Season: Summer, fall
Pleasers and teasers: Off leash, creek, lake, no fleas, views, wildflowers, golden aspens in fall; hot, dusty, exposed stretches, sections of rocky terrain under paw, sharing sections of the trail with ATVs
Map: USGS Bloody Mountain
Information: Inyo National Forest, Mammoth Ranger District, (760) 924-5500, *www.fs.fed.us/r5/inyo*, *www.visitmammoth.com*

Getting there: From the town of Mammoth Lakes, drive 2.5 miles east on Highway 203 to Highway 395. Drive 1 mile south on Highway 395 and take a right onto Sherwin Creek Road. Drive 1.5 miles on Sherwin Creek Road to the Laurel Lakes trailhead parking area.

On the trail: This 2500-foot climb over 5 miles of trail is only for very fit, hardcore hikers and their extremely fit dogs. It's scenic, it's long, and it's tough. The vegetation along the driest sections is high-desert brush. The summer months bring wildflowers to the meadows and raging waters pouring out of Laurel Lakes into aspen-lined Laurel Creek. If you hike in the summer, head up the trail at sunrise. But it's best to wait for the cooler temperatures of fall when the aspens burst into gold.

The main trail is actually a four-wheel-drive dirt and gravel—at times precarious—road that climbs and winds almost relentlessly for about 5 miles above Laurel Creek before switchbacking for 0.25 mile to the lakes. Expect to occasionally share this road with fishermen in their four-wheel-drive vehicles or ATVs.

Within 0.25 mile of stepping onto the trail, you enjoy good views of Mammoth Mountain and the surrounding ranges cradling the Owens Valley. The views become more dramatic with each foot of elevation.

A lovely hiker-friendly and less dusty alternate to the four-wheel-drive route comes into view at just over 2 miles. Watch for a fencepost just off the trail at the edge of the aspens and the creek. This is a narrow

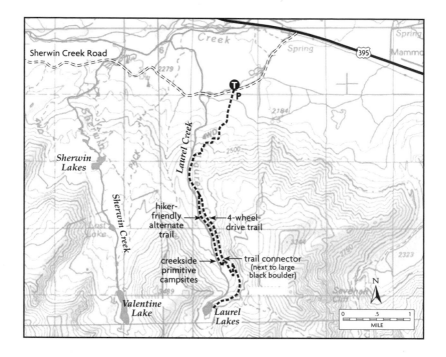

clearing and your first easy access to the flatter, splash-friendly creekside trail. The trail winds up the canyon below the main four-wheel-drive road and alongside wide-open meadows with a backdrop of towering peaks and a cascade of water tumbling out of the Laurel Lakes basin above. The creek remains within earshot or sight for the rest of the hike. At approximately 3.5 miles, the trail intersects a wide gravel access road off the main four-wheel-drive road that leads to a couple of creekside primitive campsites.

At this junction, keep your eyes open for a narrower, less obvious path, next to a large black boulder, that connects to the four-wheel-drive road about 50 feet above you. This trail connector is more obvious on your return from the lakes.

On the shore of Laurel Lake

A clue that it's time for you to return to the four-wheel-drive road above is the increasing gap between the creek and the road, as the road climbs steadily and more steeply along a seemingly endless switchback.

This is where you want to reconsider going the distance if your dog is showing signs of fatigue or paw tenderness. The next 1.25 miles are relentlessly grueling, dry, and rough under paw. Remember that once at the top of the 10,000-foot climb, you still have a 0.25-mile stretch of rough trail down to the lake. What goes down will have to come up. Make sure you have plenty of water left for your dog.

The last 0.5 mile before the downhill turnoff to the lakes levels out to phenomenal views and a spot of dark blue water, the smallest of the Laurel Lakes. The larger of the Laurel Lakes at the base of Laurel Mountain appears on your right during the descent to the lakeshore. After a rest, a snack, and a footbath in the invigorating glacial waters, the short trek back up to the main road won't be as daunting as you might dread.

A tired Stanley gets carried during the return from Laurel Lakes

Once back on the jeep road, retrace your steps and savor the amazing views along the relatively easier downhill journey back. Make a left off the four-wheel-drive road at the primitive campsite cutoff and enjoy the pleasant creekside meadow alternative until the last merge with the road in the aspen grove below.

A Cautionary Tale from the Hiking Annals

On their first visit to Laurel Lakes, two very fit people, one relatively fit person, and two perky and experienced hiking dogs, a terrier and a golden, left the trailhead with a lot of water and snacks and a checklist of essentials. They took frequent rest stops and dips in the stream and paced their stride to the less fit of the hikers. The relatively fit but extremely tired person wisely opted to end her hike at the 0.25-mile downhill turn-off to the lakes with her terrier, also in need of a rest. The two very fit hikers pressed on to the lakes with the exuberant golden fixated on a swim below. The challenging and rewarding day seemed like it would conclude without a hitch, until the terrier's gait began to show signs of tender tootsies on the return to the trailhead. No dog bootie store in sight, the hikers took turns carrying the terrier for the last couple of miles. Luckily for them, it was a cooperative fifteen-pound terrier and not an eighty-pound golden.

33. Rainbow Falls ✓

Round-trip: 6.44 miles, OB
Hiking time: 3.5–4.5 hours
Elevation range: 7203–7680 feet
Difficulty: Easy to moderate
Season: Summer, fall
Pleasers and teasers: Partial off leash, river, no fleas, views, unusual geology; mosquitoes in summer
Maps: USGS Mammoth Mountain, USGS Crystal Crag
Information: Fee; Inyo National Forest, Mammoth Ranger District, (760) 924-5500, *www.fs.fed.us/r5/inyo*, *www.visitmammoth.com*

Getting there: From the town of Mammoth Lakes off Highway 395, take the Mammoth Lakes/Highway 203 turnoff and drive 3.5 miles west

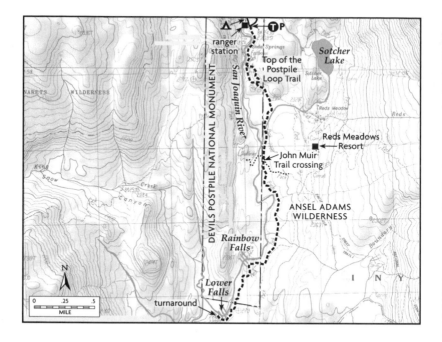

through town. Turn right on Highway 203/Minaret Road and drive 5 miles, passing Mammoth Mountain Ski Resort to the ranger booth at Minaret Vista Summit. From Minaret Vista Summit, drive 7 miles down to the Middle Fork of the San Joaquin River and Devils Postpile National Monument. Turn right at the sign for Devils Postpile. Drive 0.5 mile to the ranger station and trailhead parking lot.

During the busier summer months (June–September), only campers and backpackers are allowed to drive their vehicles beyond Minaret Vista Summit after 7:00 AM. Day hikers must drive past Minaret Vista before 7:00 AM or board the shuttle down to Devils Postpile. Call (760) 924-5500 for shuttle schedule and day use and camping fees.

On the trail: The panoramic views of peaks and the Minaret Range along the ridge and across the Middle Fork of the San Joaquin River are some of the most spectacular you will see from a car in the Sierra. This stunning high-country hamlet is loaded with unique and remarkable attributes. The paved road access is a phenomenon in itself in the heart of this pristine backcountry, wedged in a glacial fold between the eastern and western slopes of the Sierra. Then there's the geological wonder of the 60-foot-high hexagonal basalt lava columns—Devils Postpile—and the

Rainbow Falls

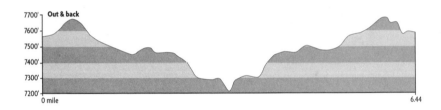

fact that dogs are just as welcome as hikers in the national monument. This is just a perk along the mostly level, dusty pumice trail leading to the main attraction, Rainbow Falls. Be aware that you share the trail with horses and pack animals.

Begin the hike behind the ranger station at the map board and follow the sign for Devils Postpile. From the parking area to Rainbow Falls, the trail descends in such a gentle, gradual slope—with the exception of a couple of slight inclines—that you will be fooled into thinking it's a level trail until your return trip, which accounts for the "moderate" part of the rating.

A wide-open meadow and the meandering-to-raging San Joaquin River (depending on snowpack and time of year) are on your right as you enter the monument about 0.25 mile in. Dogs must be leashed anytime you are in the national monument. Pass the sign on your left for the Postpile Loop Trail and continue down the main trail just past the obvious postpile. You will see another sign for the trail to the left for the "Top of the Postpile." I recommend that you and pooch take this jaunt to the top of the postpile on your way back from the falls, and follow it down to where the loop merges back onto the main trail at that first sign.

The river is within earshot or sight all the way to the falls. Watch for the posted regulation signs where the trail passes through the monument-designated land from time to time. Once outside the boundary of the monument, just past the John Muir Trail crossing, dogs can be off leash until you reach Rainbow Falls, which is also within the national monument.

As you approach the falls, notice the fire-ravaged landscape and the result of the lightning strike of 1992 that decimated close to 9000 acres, a testimony to Mother Nature's fierce temperament. Enter the Ansel Adams Wilderness after the second footbridge and come up to the sign for Rainbow Falls to the right. The trail steps down to a couple of viewing balconies for a closer look at the falls and the water-carved gorge.

To continue to Lower Falls, 0.5 mile farther and outside of the national monument boundary (code word for off leash), make a left at the "Trail to Base" sign just past the horse hitching rack. Lower Falls is an abrupt cascade draping over large granite boulders. A primitive trail drops down to the inviting pool at the base of the cascade, which is unquestionably the doggie pot of gold at the end of the "Rainbow" Falls.

Retrace your steps from the falls back to Devils Postpile. If you or pooch are not up to the hike back to the ranger station, you have the option of catching the shuttle at Reds Meadow Resort—a backcountry oasis of cabins, with a supply store, restaurant, and pack station—at the end of the paved road and the shuttle route. Watch for the spur trail sign on your right for "Resort."

34. Minaret Falls

Round-trip: 2.72 miles, OB
Hiking time: 2 hours
Elevation range: 7550–7691 feet
Difficulty: Easy, less fit okay
Season: Summer, fall
Pleasers and teasers: Partial off leash, river, shade, no fleas; mosquitoes in summer
Map: USGS Mammoth Mountain
Information: Fee; Inyo National Forest, Mammoth Ranger District, (760) 924-5500, *www.fs.fed.us/r5/inyo, www.visitmammoth.com*

Getting there: From the town of Mammoth Lakes off Highway 395, take the Mammoth Lakes/Highway 203 turnoff and drive 3.5 miles west through town. Turn right on Highway 203/Minaret Road and drive 5 miles, passing Mammoth Mountain Ski Resort to the ranger booth at Minaret Vista Summit. From Minaret Vista Summit, drive 7 miles down to the Middle Fork of the San Joaquin River and Devils Postpile National Monument. Turn right at the sign for Devils Postpile. Drive 0.5 mile to the ranger station and trailhead parking lot.

During the busier summer months (June–September), only campers and backpackers are allowed to drive their vehicles beyond Minaret Vista Summit after 7:00 AM. Day hikers must drive past Minaret Vista before 7:00 AM or board the shuttle down to Devils Postpile. Call (760) 924-5500 for shuttle schedule and day use and camping fees.

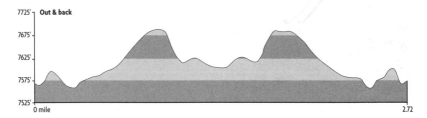

On the trail: What this hike doesn't boast in grandiose views, it makes up for with a level, pine-shaded route between the backside of the western Sierra slopes and the prominent Middle Fork of the San Joaquin River. The trail leads you to the base of the surprisingly underrated Minaret Falls and the opportunity to hike along one of the country's most famous trails, the Pacific Crest. Watch for national monument–posted regulations in the initial stretch of this hike, where pooch must be leashed from time to time. These brief interruptions to his sprints of wild abandon are good opportunities to practice recall drills and will make off-leash romping farther along the hike even sweeter.

Begin your hike in the Devils Postpile parking area behind the ranger station and follow the trail to Devils Postpile. Take a right at the intersection onto the Minaret Falls Trail, and cross the arched footbridge over the San Joaquin River. Continue along the trail until it intersects the John Muir and Pacific Crest trails. Expect to see some serious and heavily loaded backpackers journeying along this trail. Turn right onto the Pacific Crest

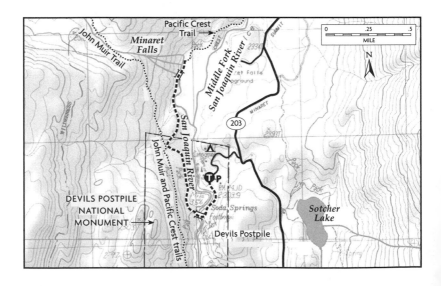

Minaret Falls

Trail to Minaret Falls, whose flow will become increasingly louder until you reach the twin log footbridge. Halfway across the footbridge, the view corridor of the falls opens up between the lush curtains of green. Just ahead and past the footbridge are spur trails that lead to the gigantic boulders and slabs of granite beneath the falls, more of them become exposed and are perfect for lounging, picnicking, and scrambling late in the season as the snowmelt wanes and the flow relaxes. Retrace your steps, paying attention to the trail intersection and the left turn back across the San Joaquin River.

35. Panorama Dome ✓

Round-trip: 0.83 mile, OB
Hiking time: 1 hour
Elevation range: 8670–8905 feet
Difficulty: Easy, less fit okay
Season: Late spring, summer, fall
Pleasers and teasers: Off leash, no fleas, views
Map: USGS Crystal Crag
Information: Inyo National Forest, Mammoth Ranger District,
    (760) 924-5500, *www.fs.fed.us/r5/inyo, www.visitmammoth.com*

Getting there: From the town of Mammoth Lakes off Highway 395, take the Mammoth Lakes/ Highway 203 turnoff and drive 3.5 miles west through town to the Highway 203/Minaret Road and Lake Mary Road junction. Continue straight on Lake Mary Road 2.5 miles to the Panorama

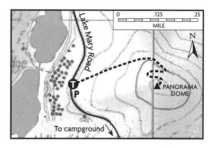

Dome trailhead. The trailhead is on the left side of Lake Mary Road with limited roadside parking. There is also room for a couple of cars on the right side of the road across from the discreet trailhead and its narrow tree-lined trail.

On the trail: At first glance, this hike seems too short and convenient to hold any promise of reward. Start with a gentle uphill along this forested trail, following the path to where it emerges from the trees to the open meadow at the top. To Rover, this is just another opportunity to scamper around. But there isn't another hike in these parts where you can be so wowed by the views with so little sweat. Feast on the 360-degree panorama. From this perspective, Mammoth Mountain seems so close you could almost reach out and touch it. The dome is a scenic lookout over the town of Mammoth Lakes, with views of the White Mountains and Crowley Lake in the distance, embraced by Mammoth Mountain and the Mammoth Crest above and Twin Lakes below. When you're finished gorging on the views, retrace your steps back down the trail to your vehicle.

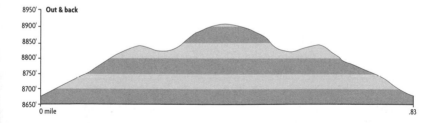

Opposite: Alex explores atop Panorama Dome, with a view of Crystal Crag and Mammoth Crest.

36. Horseshoe Lake ✓

Round-trip: 1.62 miles, L
Hiking time: 1.5 hours
Elevation range: 8949–9018 feet
Difficulty: Easy, less fit okay
Season: Summer, fall
Pleasers and teasers: Off leash, lake, shade, no fleas, good acclimatization trail; slopes by the parking lot defaced by stands of dead trees as a result of carbon dioxide poisoning, mosquitoes in summer
Map: USGS Crystal Crag
Information: Inyo National Forest, Mammoth Ranger District, (760) 924-5500, *www.fs.fed.us/r5/inyo*, *www.visitmammoth.com*

Getting there: From the town of Mammoth Lakes off Highway 395, drive west to the Highway 203/Minaret Road and Lake Mary Road junction. Continue straight on Lake Mary Road for 5 miles to the Horseshoe Lake parking lot.

On the trail: The carbon dioxide phenomenon in this part of the lake's basin doesn't create a very pretty first impression of Horseshoe Lake. As you approach the parking lot and look to the right of Horseshoe Lake, the scenery is rather eerie. The gray, naked limbs of the tall pine trees clinging to the dusty slopes of Mammoth Pass are reminiscent of the kind of natural devastation you might expect after nuclear war. Although the carbon dioxide-damaged trees aren't exactly eye candy, this a rare opportunity to witness up close the fascinating geological activity in this area and is just one of several reasons to hike here. Somehow that doesn't seem to interfere with your dog's enjoyment of the lake and trail.

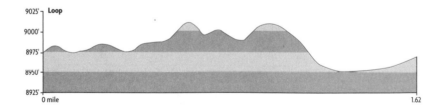

Spencer and Alex lead the way on the flat trail around Horseshoe Lake.

Taking a rest after the hike around Horseshoe Lake

The trail begins at the end of the paved parking area between the lake and the carbon dioxide-scarred stand of trees. Signs are posted around the parking lot and on the bathrooms explaining the death of the trees,

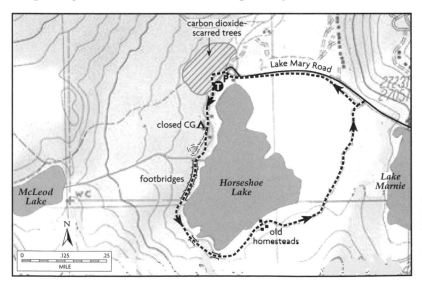

which is believed to have been caused by a shallow intrusion of magma that triggered a release of carbon dioxide in 1989. Horseshoe Lake is also known unofficially as "Dog Lake" because of the number of local and visiting dogs who come and play on its shores.

The trailhead sign has a map showing the mountain bike trail around the lake and beyond. You will be sharing this trail with other hikers, dogs, and cyclists but mostly with other hikers and their dogs. Follow the well-worn, exposed trail toward the healthier green forest with the lake on your left. The trail contours most of the lake a few yards above the shore through a pine forest and crosses seasonal ribbons of water on several wooden footbridges. Just before the trail begins to curve around the lake, it veers away from the lake onto a wider double-track bike path. Continue along this path, passing the remains of a couple of old homestead foundations. The lake is on your left even if it disappears from sight occasionally. The trail eventually Ts into Lake Mary Road, but a narrower trail paralleling Lake Mary Road turns left toward Horseshoe Lake and the parking lot.

37. McLeod Lake ✓

Round-trip: 1.77 miles, SL
Hiking time: 2 hours
Difficulty: Easy to moderate
Elevation range: 8990–9329 feet
Season: Summer, fall
Pleasers and teasers: Off leash, lake, shade, no fleas, solitude; mosquitoes in summer
Map: USGS Crystal Crag
Information: Inyo National Forest, Mammoth Ranger District, (760) 924-5500, *www.fs.fed.us/r5/inyo, www.visitmammoth.com*

Getting there: From the town of Mammoth Lakes off Highway 395, drive west to the Highway 203/Minaret Road and Lake Mary Road junction. Continue straight on Lake Mary Road for 5 miles to the Horseshoe Lake parking lot.

On the trail: On rare and far between occasions in life, a situation comes along that seems too good to be true, but turns out to be true. The hike

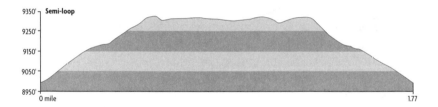

to McLeod Lake is one of those. It's a short and relatively easy jaunt to one of the most pristine and lightly frequented settings in the Eastern Sierra. The first thoughts triggered by McLeod Lake: how can you walk to something this pretty from a paved parking lot and with so little exertion, and where is everybody? What you see is what you get, honest!

Begin at the sign for Mammoth Pass. The moonscape trail climbs gently into greener pine forest. The first sign on the trail notifies hikers that permits are necessary for overnight camping. Farther up you'll come to a trail sign arrow pointing to McLeod Lake to the left and Mammoth Pass and Reds Meadow to the right. Go left and follow the trail to McLeod Lake. The trail levels off at a junction for Red Cones and Upper Meadow to the left and Mammoth Pass and Reds Meadow Trail to the right. You can see McLeod Lake on your left through the trees.

Walk to the shoreline and soak in the quiet beauty of your surroundings. On a summer weekend, you may see a couple of fishermen float tubing on the lake. The grouping of granite boulders at the lake's south

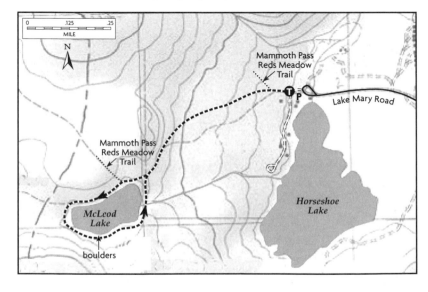

Alex cools off at McLeod Lake.

shore across the way makes a great picnic perch. Turn right to follow the trail around the lake. The lake flows out and cascades down toward Horseshoe Lake near the close of your lake loop. The vegetation may make it difficult to see the outflow and the path across it, but stay close to the lakeshore and you will see large fallen tree limbs that bridge the shallow moving water for a dry crossing. Once around the lake, retrace your steps to the parking lot.

38. Emerald Lake

Round-trip: 1.5 miles, OB
Hiking time: 1.5–2 hours
Elevation range: 9120–9540 feet
Difficulty: Easy
Season: Summer, fall
Pleasers and teasers: Off leash, lake, shade, no fleas, views; mosquitoes in summer
Map: USGS Bloody Mountain
Information: Inyo National Forest, Mammoth Ranger District, (760) 924-5500, *www.fs.fed.us/r5/inyo, www.visitmammoth.com*

Getting there: From the town of Mammoth Lakes off Highway 395, drive west to the Highway 203/Minaret Road and Lake Mary Road junction. Continue straight on Lake Mary Road for 3.5 miles and turn left at Lake Mary. Drive 0.5 mile to Coldwater Creek campground and turn left into the campground. Drive 0.5 mile to the Emerald Lake trailhead parking lot at the far end of the campground.

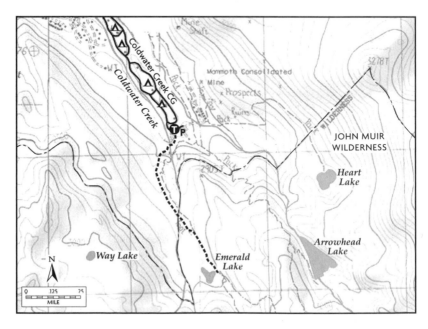

Dakota and Chitsa at Emerald Lake

Keep your dog on leash when you encounter horses on the trail.

On the trail: This is a short and sweet jaunt with just the right combination of cardio workout, flowing water, shade, and views to satisfy both dogs and hikers.

The trailhead is to the left of the stream, and the trail rises from the parking lot to parallel the stream on the right with the water tower on the left. The trail continues to rise gently with the stream always on your left and slightly below. The trail levels off just beyond the John Muir Wilderness boundary, giving you and pooch a chance to catch your breath before reaching the lakeshore. The peak views to the right are divine and continue to amaze as the Mammoth Crest wraps around Emerald Lake. Retrace your steps back to the parking lot.

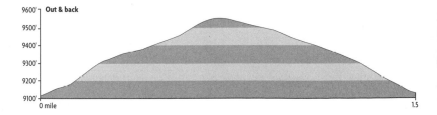

39. Crystal Lake ✓

Round-trip: 2.65 miles, OB
Hiking time: 2–3 hours
Elevation range: 9048–9736 feet
Difficulty: Moderate
Season: Summer, fall
Pleasers and teasers: Off leash, lake, shade, no fleas, views, scenic campground at trailhead; mosquitoes in summer, trail has been abused
Map: USGS Crystal Crag
Information: Inyo National Forest, Mammoth Ranger District, (760) 924-5500, *www.fs.fed.us/r5/inyo, www.visitmammoth.com*

Getting there: From the town of Mammoth Lakes off Highway 395, drive west to the Highway 203/Minaret Road and Lake Mary Road junction. Continue on Lake Mary Road for 4 miles and turn left at the west end of Lake Mary and the marina. Drive 0.5 mile along the west shore

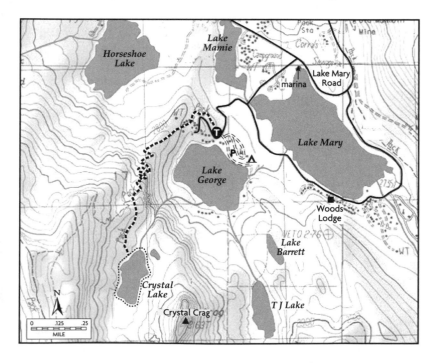

of Lake Mary and turn right going uphill to the Lake George Recreation Area parking lot.

On the trail: This is just another postcard-perfect destination in exchange for a little sweat and heavy breathing.

Facing Lake George, turn right, away from the lake and Woods Lodge, and walk down to the trailhead and map board to the left of the parking lot. Follow the dirt trail, with its intruding large roots and scattered boulders, as it starts to climb out of the parking lot, eventually switchbacking behind the cabins at Woods Lodge. Lake George soon becomes visible on your left with the Crystal Crag rock formation towering above the lake. Crystal Lake sits to the right and beneath the crag.

The trail continues to climb moderately, sometimes leveling out for a short distance along the ridgeline above Lake George. It veers away from the awesome views into more forested terrain slightly toward the backside of the ridge before zigzagging back to the ridgeline. About 0.75 mile along, the trail meets the granite-bouldered ridge that provides the grandest views of Lakes George and Mary below, as well as the imposing Mammoth Crest above.

The trail continues to switchback until it appears that your path might collide with the flat rock face ahead. Mammoth Mountain rises to your right. Resist the temptation to follow in the bootsteps of hikers who have created a confusing maze of trails by cutting off the switchbacks. You'll know you are still on course when the trail cuts between the backside of the ridge on your left and the granite face on your right. Walk past the sign for Mammoth Crest and continue on the main trail to Crystal Lake. The trail levels off at 9736 feet, facing Crystal Crag. Follow the meandering trail toward the sound of the water spilling out of Crystal Lake into Lake George.

There's a primitive trail around the lake with picnic-perfect boulders. Circling the lake counterclockwise requires some fancy footwork over fallen trees and granite escarpments. A safer and equally rewarding

Lakeshore boulders at Crystal Lake are the perfect spot for a well-earned rest.

option is to walk across the lake's outlet at the foot of the trail and hike the lakeshore clockwise along the granite boulders to the meadow at the base of the crest.

When you're ready, retrace your steps to the trail that brought you down to the lake's outlet. Once you're back on the ridge, the trail will be easy to identify and follow back to the parking lot.

Dakota on the rocky Crystal Lake Trail

40. Convict Lake Loop

Round-trip: 2.55 miles, L
Hiking time: 1.5–2 hours
Difficulty: Easy to moderate, less fit okay
Elevation range: 7588–7812 feet
Season: Summer, fall
Pleasers and teasers: Off leash, lake, shade, no fleas, views; mosquitoes in summer, busy on summer weekends
Maps: USGS Convict Lake, USGS Bloody Mountain
Information: Inyo National Forest, Mammoth Ranger District, (760) 924-5500, *www.fs.fed.us/r5/inyo, www.visitmammoth.com*

Getting there: From the town of Mammoth Lakes, drive 4.5 miles south along Highway 395 and turn right at the Convict Lake turnoff. Drive 2 miles and turn left at the lake for the day-use parking area.

On the trail: Convict Lake is a mile-long, 138-foot-deep glacial lake nestled in a bowl, also known as a tarn, at the base of the moraine and probably the most dramatic high-country lake setting you will ever drive to.

Begin your hike by walking to the far end of the parking lot and turning left onto a paved pathway that takes you across the road to another

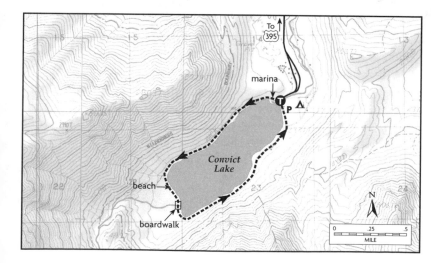

Dramatic scenery at Convict Lake

paved walkway along the lake's edge. The pathway may be obscured by the sagebrush growing along the parking lot and the paths, but keep an eye to the left of the parking area as you walk and you will see it drop to the left.

Once across the road and on the path, go right in a counterclockwise direction around the lake, past the marina and the boathouse to the trailhead at the end of the parking area. The trail parallels the lake and on this side is bordered by some aspens but mostly by high-desert sage and bitterbrush.

The terrain around the lake undulates from the shoreline up to about seventy feet high at its farthest from the water but offers several opportunities for your dog to catch a dip where the trail kisses the shoreline.

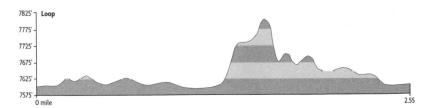

The high mountain scenery as you look down the trail is almost hypnotic and interrupted only by glimpses of fishing boats and bobbing float tubers on the clear surface of the lake.

After the first mile, the trail divides. Bear left and follow the fishermen and hiker trail. As you reach the opposite end of the lake, the terrain becomes marshier and the trail goes along a 500-foot section of boardwalk. You can see the marina straight across the lake from this point. Follow the trail under the aspen canopy, watching for the root obstacle course before emerging from the trees and climbing about twelve railroad tie steps. You've contoured the lake's inlet and are looping back toward the parking lot. Notice the contrast between the southerly exposed arid landscape and the northerly exposed leafy green slopes.

As you approach the close of the loop, you will see a gravel point of beach reaching into the lake and a paved path for "foot traffic only," where you'll find several benches and a picnic table tucked idyllically under the trees. The path ends almost directly across from the parking lot, facing the lake with several historical and geological information plaques. Mount Morrison rises on the left. The mountain was named after Sheriff Robert Morrison, who, in 1871 headed the posse chasing the Carson City jail escapees to Convict Lake. The highest peak on the right is Laurel Mountain, which has the distinction of having some of the oldest rocks—aged at 4 million years old—in the Sierra Nevada.

41. McGee Creek ✓

Round-trip: 7.33 miles, OB
Hiking time: 3.5–4.5 hours
Elevation range: 7836–9235 feet
Difficulty: Easy to moderate
Season: Summer, fall
Pleasers and teasers: Off leash, creek, no fleas, views; mosquitoes in summer
Map: USGS Convict Lake
Information: Inyo National Forest, Mammoth Ranger District, (760) 924-5500, *www.fs.fed.us/r5/inyo, www.visitmammoth.com*

Getting there: From the town of Mammoth Lakes, drive 8 miles south along Highway 395 to the McGee Creek turnoff on the right. Follow the

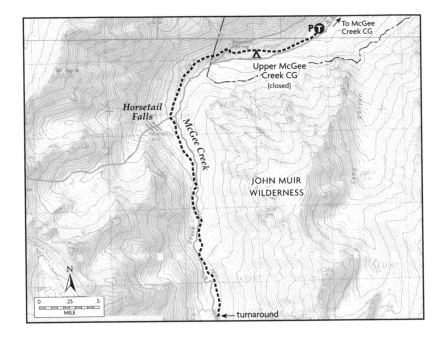

road 3 miles up to the trailhead parking. The first 2 miles are paved; the last mile is gravel.

On the trail: McGee Creek trailhead is a jumping-off point for a couple of arduous high-country lakes. But the first 3 moderately strenuous miles along the creek provide enough diversity, fun, and scenery for a leisurely half-day excursion with pooch. You cross an open, high-desert plain transitioning to aspen groves and meadows on the way to a lazy stretch of the creek tucked in a sunny gorge.

The hike begins at the far end of the parking lot along a wide, coarse dirt trail that was once a road to Upper McGee Creek campground, which is now closed. McGee Creek flows vigorously to the left of the trail behind a lush curtain of aspens. Although the creek remains in sight for

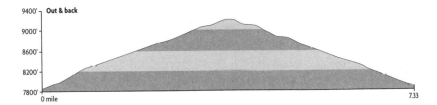

the entire hike, it will often be several feet below the trail and rushing by too tumultuously for pooch to enjoy. Bring enough water to weather the summer sun, which can be punishing by late morning.

As you leave the open plain, the trail ascends gradually into the swales streaked with wide, sweeping brushstrokes of aspens and green, leafy berry bushes on this grandiose canvas of peaks, boulders, and pine-dotted

Everyone carries their load.

slopes. After a few switchbacks climbing to the right, you enter the John Muir Wilderness and trade sagebrush for fields of mule's ear plants, tall grasses, and blossoming bushes. Horsetail Falls appears on the face of the palisades in the distance to your right, soon spilling its waters across the trail. Early in the season, the volume is enough to warrant switching to river sandals.

The trail continues to climb steadily, eventually leveling off as you emerge from the narrows of the canyon where the creek seems to funnel out between the talus slopes and briefly comes in contact with the edge of the trail. Continue along a talus-covered, dry streambed, evidence of past slides and erosion. Cross the stream along a wooden-plank footbridge. The creek is now on your right traversing a lovely meadow. Press on just a little farther until you reach another footbridge where the hasty flow is interrupted by a flat, shallow pool rimmed in the summer by a small but inviting stretch of sandy beach on either side of the bridge. Retrace your steps back to the parking lot.

42. Gem Lakes

Round-trip: 6.83 miles, OB
Hiking time: 4–5 hours, or overnight at Gem Lakes
Elevation range: 10,305–10,977 feet
Difficulty: Moderate
Season: Summer, fall
Pleasers and teasers: Off leash, lake, no fleas, views, good overnight; mosquitoes in summer, parking lot fills early on weekends and holidays
Maps: USGS Mount Morgan, USGS Mount Abbot
Information: Inyo National Forest, White Mountain Ranger District, (760) 873-2500, *www.fs.fed.us/r5/inyo*

Getting there: From the town of Mammoth Lakes, drive 15 miles south on Highway 395 to the Rock Creek turnoff on the right. Drive 9 miles up the Rock Creek canyon and continue another mile past the Rock Creek Resort and Pack Station bearing left along the main but narrower road to the Mosquito Flats parking lot. The 10-mile scenic drive from Highway 395 to the trailhead along the rushing creek is a treat in itself.

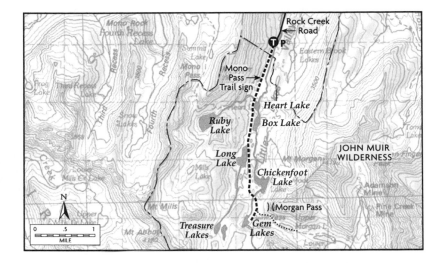

On the trail: This hike is a series of alpine meadows interlaced with streams and lakes galore in exchange for a few moderate inclines and the likely lightheadedness that comes with beginning a jaunt at 10,000 feet. Just remember to savor it slowly. Walk to the far end of the parking lot, past the bathroom on your right and the footbridge on your left, onto the wide, mostly hard-packed dirt trail.

The trail begins with a steady and gradual incline transitioning from dirt to large granite stepping-stones bridging some of the seasonal ribbons of water. The steepest part of this fairly level trail is behind you as you enter the John Muir Wilderness. Continue along the main trail toward Gem Lakes at the sign for Gem Lakes ahead or Mono Pass to the right.

From here, the trail undulates toward the snowcapped mountainous backdrop, interrupted by streams, meadows, and sparkling lakes. The easy access to such stunning high-country scenery and its relatively level terrain makes this one of the most popular hikes in the Eastern Sierra. Your dog will swoon with pleasure inhaling the meadow smells and lurching at the sounds of chirping chipmunks.

The large lake on your left is Heart Lake, where the trail narrows and veers away from the water through a tree-lined meadow until it emerges above the far end of the lake. Shortly, you'll reach another plateau and Long Lake, which stretches toward the base of the snow-covered peaks, giving you the impression of walking into a postcard. The trail follows most of the shoreline of Long Lake in the shadow of a rock wall on your left.

The trail gently rises above the lake and continues past the Chickenfoot Lake trailhead on your left below the moraine slopes. Just before the next and final rise on your hike to Gem Lakes, you will catch a glimpse of Chickenfoot Lake through the trees on your left.

Lucky for you, most hikers make Chickenfoot Lake their destination. Continuing along the trail, you reach the trail sign for Morgan Pass and Gem Lakes. Turn right to Gem Lakes and some of the shallow boulder and flat rock-strewn ponds will come into view, an irresistible attraction for splash-happy canines. The trail crisscrosses to the last spit of land, boulders, and stunted pines overlooking the lake beneath the sawtooth ridge rising like a sentinel over this pristine domain.

The aquamarine shades of this larger lake rival the palette of Caribbean waters, glistening like a precious gemstone. This is the end of the rainbow and a picture-perfect rest and picnic stop.

Retrace your steps from the Gem Lakes basin back to the main trail and down to the parking lot.

Off-trail Perks

If you and your dog are into creature comforts, the Mammoth area abounds with dog-friendly housekeeping cabins where you can walk out the door and onto the trail for the day and return to cozy comforts at night. These include Crystal Crag Lodge at Lake Mary, Woods Lodge at Lake George, Red's Meadow Lodge, Convict Lake Lodge, and Rock Creek Lodge.

Rock Creek Resort makes up for not allowing pets in their cabins with fresh-baked pies (they sell out early and fast). Stop at Schatz Bakery in Mammoth Lakes or Bishop for trail goodies. In Mammoth Lakes, Gomez Mexican Restaurant and its outdoor patio, with shade for pooch, hits the spot after a day on the trail.

Opposite: Stanley rests at a trail intersection sign on the way to Gem Lakes.

BISHOP

43. Chocolate Lakes Loop

Round-trip: 6.39 miles, SL; 4 miles to Long Lake, OB
Hiking time: 4–5 hours for SL; 2.5–3 hours for OB, or overnight at
the third Chocolate Lake or Bull Lake
Elevation range: 9836–11,331 feet
Difficulty: Moderate to strenuous
Season: Summer, fall
Pleasers and teasers: Off leash, lake, shade, no fleas, views, good
overnight; mosquitoes in summer, parking lot fills early in summer
Map: USGS Mount Thompson
Information: Inyo National Forest, White Mountain Ranger District,
(760) 873-2500, *www.fs.fed.us/r5/inyo*

Getting there: From downtown Bishop driving south on Highway 395,
turn right onto Highway 168/West Line Street. Drive 15 miles to the South
Lake turnoff. Turn left and drive 7 miles to the South Lake parking lot
and trailhead at the end of the road.

On the trail: This hike, in the granite belly of the High Sierra spires,
climbs like a stairway to the heavens, where lakes are jewels crowned by
meadows and peaks, each emerging vista more intoxicating than the last.
The trail begins at South Lake and climbs steadily along Bishop Pass Trail
to Long Lake, briefly but steeply to Ruwau Lake, briefly and even more
steeply to the ridge above Chocolate Lakes, ending with a sure-footed rock
scramble down to the first Chocolate Lake shore before meandering past
the second and third Chocolate Lake, and finally along Bull Lake before
completing the loop down along the Bishop Pass Trail back to the parking

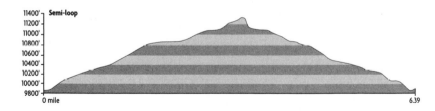

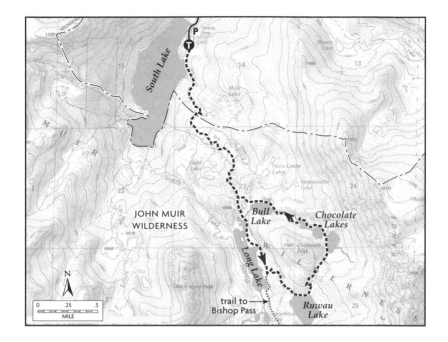

lot. The catch is the potentially heart- and head-thumping altitude, the steep 2.5-mile sprints between Long and Ruwau lakes, and Ruwau to the ridge above Chocolate Lakes, and that downhill rock scramble finale.

If you are fit and acclimated and your dog is a seasoned hiker in his prime, this loop will be a long-lasting hiking memory. If either or both of you don't quite make the "fitness" cut for the loop this time, the hike to Long Lake and back is significantly less strenuous but no less rewarding in beauty and frolic.

Mostly paw friendly, the trail is loose dirt interspersed with a series of granite stepping slabs as it climbs steadily and at times relentlessly between level breath-catching stretches. Just past the sign for the John Muir Wilderness is a smaller sign for Bishop Pass and Treasure Lakes. Bear left to Bishop Pass. Farther up, at the sign for Bishop Pass or Bull Lake, continue your journey toward Bishop Pass and note that if you opt for the loop, you will be rejoining the trail from Bull Lake at this intersection.

As you approach Long Lake, you are about to be wowed by the postcard-perfect setting of this long, deep, clear lake below the snow-patched granite cirque above. At Long Lake, you must decide whether to goof off along this divine mile-long stretch of lakeside trail before heading back or to press upward and onward along the loop route. If you have any doubts about your—and especially your dog's—stamina reserves, not to mention the condition of his paws, make a day of Long Lake.

For those prepared with water, snacks, and energy to burn, continue along the east side of Long Lake and take the strenuous spur trail left up the log steps at the sign for Ruwau Lake. The incline tapers off at a meadow and Ruwau Lake sits at the base of a talus slope. Continue along the trail hugging the north shore of the lake and forge on through some slightly overgrown sections of trail until you see an unmarked but worn spur trail veering left up the slope across the small pine-studded island just offshore. This next 0.5 mile of rugged, rocky terrain leads to a ridge above Chocolate Lakes and marks the beginning of your return loop. The trail is a bit of a scramble, occasionally requiring some hand-over-hand technique. Steer your route slightly to the right as you approach the top where it drops down to a saddle. You'll get a disappointingly stark glimpse

Spring flowers along the Chocolate Lakes Trail

of the first of the three Chocolate Lakes en route. The hike down to the edge of the first lake is the next and last challenging hurdle. There is no single definitive trail, just a lot of rock and traces of trails where other hikers have negotiated their way down to the water's edge. Once at the lake, follow the trail on the west shore, staying as close as possible to the water through some overgrown vegetation.

Once you reach the far end of the lake, it just keeps getting better. The gigantic boulder in the middle of the trail between the first and second Chocolate Lake is a perfect snack and rest stop and viewing platform to scan the panorama beyond. From here the trail leads you east of the third Chocolate Lake around the far end and down toward Bull Lake, another destination in its own right. Stay on the trail to circle on the west and north shore of Bull Lake as it descends from the plateau and rejoins the main trail at the trail junction for Bishop Pass and Bull Lake. Make a right on the trail and retrace your route down to the parking lot at South Lake.

44. Grass Lake ✓

Round-trip: 3.81 miles, OB
Hiking time: 2.5–3 hours
Elevation range: 9261–9937 feet
Difficulty: Easy
Season: Summer, fall
Pleasers and teasers: Off leash, lake, shade, no fleas, views; mosquitoes in summer, parking is 0.5 mile from trailhead
Map: USGS Mount Darwin
Information: Inyo National Forest, White Mountain Ranger District, (760) 873-2500, *www.fs.fed.us/r5/inyo*

Getting there: From downtown Bishop driving south on Highway 395, turn right onto Highway 168/West Line Street. Drive 18 miles and make a right turn on the first road immediately after the Sabrina Basin and hiker parking sign. This is the road to North Lake. Drive 1.5 miles on a partially paved and gravel road to the Bishop Pack Outfitter station. The road is well traveled and maintained, but it is narrow with a steep dropoff and a couple of blind curves as it winds up to the top. Turn right at the Bishop Pack Outfitter sign, just before the North Lake Campground and

Alex and Moses cross a stream on the way to Grass Lake.

"Fee Area No Day Use" sign. The trailhead is in the North Lake campground, 0.5 mile past the pack outfitter. There is no day-use parking in the campground, and that rule is enforced.

The pack outfitter corrals will be on the left and parking lot number 1 is just in front. If that lot is full, continue past the pack outfitter to lot number 2. Walk back to the main gravel road, turn right, and continue 0.5 mile to the Grass Lake trailhead at the far right end of the North Lake campground by a large National Forest Service map and information board.

On the trail: The trail begins as a sandy path bordered by lush greenery most of the summer as it passes by a few campsites before coming to another trail signpost for Piute Pass to the right and Grass Lake and Lamarck Lakes to the left. This is an enchanting hike requiring moderate exertion as you wind your way up to an idyllic, grassy meadow complete with lake, wetland habitat, and picnic boulders cradled by a craggy crest and scree slopes.

The trail crosses three footbridges before ascending a series of moderate switchbacks through the boulder-strewn pine trees and up some rocky

Grass Lake provides an ideal place for dogs to play.

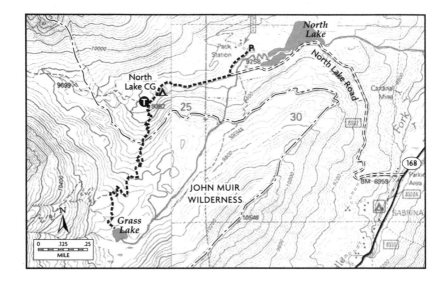

steps. The trail levels on a plateau before the next series of switchbacks. You will see a sign for Lamarck Lakes to the right and Grass Lake straight ahead. Stay on the trail heading to Grass Lake and take a moment to look back for a glimpse across Owens Valley through the trees. The trail levels off and descends gently, and soon the sound of flowing water will float up on your right as the trail unveils the green meadow below and its backdrop of pine-dotted, scree-draped slopes.

Once at the lake, your dog will find the best access for frolicking in the water in a splash. Walk to your right along the shoreline and follow the sound of the rushing water until you come to the lake's outflow with huge limbs to sit on for a pleasant snack spot.

There's something about Grass Lake that makes you want to linger. When you and pooch have nourished yourself with this power spot's serene beauty, retrace your steps to the campground and down the road to the parking lot.

45. Lake Sabrina

Round-trip: 2.36 miles, OB
Hiking time: 2.5–3 hours
Elevation range: 9137–9186 feet
Difficulty: Easy to moderate
Season: Summer, fall
Pleasers and teasers: Off leash, lake, no fleas, views; mosquitoes in summer
Map: USGS Mount Thompson
Information: Inyo National Forest, White Mountain Ranger District, (760) 873-2500, *www.fs.fed.us/r5/inyo*

Getting there: From downtown Bishop driving south on Highway 395, turn right onto Highway 168/West Line Street. Drive 19 miles to the Lake Sabrina parking lot.

On the trail: This 2.36-mile agility course for the sure-footed along the scenic north shore of Lake Sabrina will bring out the mountain goat in you and your dog. The narrow and sometimes primitive trail begins behind the fishing store and café at Lake Sabrina and ends at the west end of the lake where the creek plummets into Sabrina. Take water for your pooch as the trail traces this side of Lake Sabrina about 30 feet above

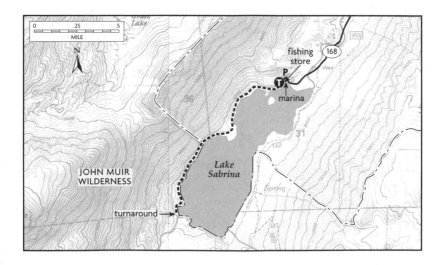

the shoreline most of the way, only occasionally dipping to the water's edge for pooch's paddling and cooling pleasure. The views are intoxicating and the rock scampering exhilarating. The lake remains in view the entire length of the hike except for a couple of short detours through the aspens or when it is screened by some overgrown clumps of vegetation or the lakeshore bluff. Beware of the wide, rock-littered slopes that bisect the dirt trail along the way.

Tired dogs heading home on the Lake Sabrina Trail

At approximately 0.5 mile, the trail transitions from a dirt path to a less-defined giant stepping-stone bridge across the flattened tower of granite dominoes. Traverse this and follow the faint gray, worn line of flatter rocks on a straight course until your boots and paws make contact with the more visibly etched dirt trail. If your dog is new to this intimidating rocky terrain, take it slow and cautious while he builds his confidence, not to mention avoids injury to his paw pads. Don't let him miss a chance for a soothing paw soak in the lake whenever the trail dips close to the water's edge. The trail end will be obvious where the glacial waters continue to carve their widening path down the rocky face of Sabrina Basin. Looking back, you will see the marina and fishing store sitting opposite from the precarious inlet crossing. That's enough adventure for one hike. Enjoy the mood-elevating therapy of the rushing water before carefully retracing your steps back to the parking lot.

Off-trail Perks

Parcher's Resort by South Lake offers dog-friendly cabins, a few RV spaces, and a country store for supplies.

BIG PINE

46. First Falls and Second Falls

Round-trip: 3.53 miles, OB
Hiking time: 3.5 hours
Elevation range: 7810–8503 feet
Difficulty: Easy to moderate
Season: Summer, fall
Pleasers and teasers: Off leash, creek, no fleas, views; mosquitoes in summer
Map: USGS Coyote Flat
Information: Inyo National Forest, White Mountain Ranger District, (760) 873-2500, *www.fs.fed.us/r5/inyo*

Getting there: From downtown Bishop, drive 15 miles south on Highway 395 to Big Pine. Turn right on Crocker Road, just after the sign for Big Pine Recreation Area. Drive 10.5 miles west on Crocker Road/Glacier

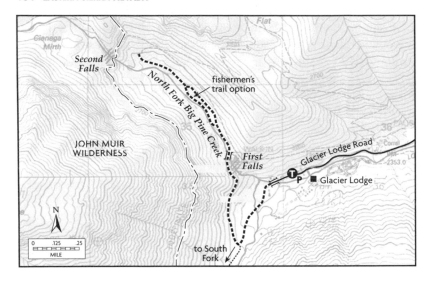

Lodge Road into the Big Pine campground parking lot at the end of the road. The trailhead is just behind the locked gate at the far end of the campground.

On the trail: At a glance, the high-desert landscape seems swept with stark aridness from the valley floor, up the hollows, to the edge of the western peaks. It comes as a surprise to be met by lush water-fed vistas behind the hostile screen of sparse and thirsty brush-covered slopes in the shadow of the icy granite sentinels. This is yet another sweet Sierra hike with a couple of wooden bridges, cascades, views, and moderate exertion.

Walk around the locked gate to the map board on the right to orient yourself. The granite cliffs that guard Palisade Glacier, the southernmost permanent glacier in North America, rise ahead beyond the white-water folds of the South Fork of Big Pine Creek on your left. Walk along the paved section of road that parallels the creek on your left and the summer cabins above on your right. The road narrows into a trail, and as you pass

Backpackers starting out on the trail to First Falls and Second Falls

the last cabin, veer right up a wider stretch of road and watch for the wooden trail sign pointing left away from the cabin road access.

Walk left up the rock steps above the creek and cross the bridge over First Falls. You'll come to a sign for South Fork, pointing left, down the expansive, flat creek bed toward the palisades. Turn right on North Fork and hike up the switchbacks on a more exposed trail of rock steps, exposing Kodak-moment views.

The trail levels off and becomes shadier with a welcome stretch of sand and mulchlike carpet under your pooch's paws. Stay on the trail, encouraging your dog to take advantage of the creek accesses on the right along this placid stretch.

You'll soon cross a second bridge. Bear left on the trail, paralleling the north fork of the creek, which is now on your left. Ignore the upper trail that climbs the slope to the right. Your trail is slightly above the creek; a fishermens trail meanders through the high-desert sage patches closer to the bank part of the way. On a warm day, the fishermens bankside trail is a cooler option for pooch's splashing pleasure until the trail veers back up to merge into the wider trail. By now Second Falls is coming into view at the far end of this sunny canyon.

When you reach what seems to be the end of the trail, veer right onto a narrow, obscure trail that gently climbs along the canyon's arid sage-covered slopes away from the creek. Keep an eye out for an unmarked, primitive spur trail to the left that threads around the manzanita bushes. Second Falls is in full view as it plunges from the plateau on the left side of the rocky backdrop. You and pooch can hang out in this open space admiring the falls from one of the boulder perches closer to the bottom, or if you feel adventurous, follow the primitive trail upward toward the rock outcropping to the right of the falls for a closer view of the cascading water and a higher perch to soak in the surrounding vistas. Watch your step around some of the sprouting cacti as you approach the rock outcropping. When you're ready, retrace your steps back to the main trail.

Off-trail Perks

A rudimentary but welcome amenity, Glacier Lodge offers rustic cabins, a store for snacks, and a grassy picnic table.

47. Bristlecone Pine Forest Discovery Trail

Round-trip: 0.81 mile, L

Hiking time: 30 minutes–1 hour

Elevation range: 10,057–10,377 feet

Difficulty: Easy, less fit okay

Season: Late spring, summer, fall

Pleasers and teasers: No fleas, unique ecological destination you can share with pooch, views; hot and dry summers, no water

Map: USGS Blanco Mountain

Information: Inyo National Forest, White Mountain Ranger District, (760) 873-2500, *www.fs.fed.us/r5/inyo*

Getting there: From downtown Bishop, drive 15 miles south on Highway 395 to Big Pine. Turn left onto Highway 168 East, 0.5 mile north of Big Pine, and drive about 13 miles along the National Forest Scenic Byway. Turn left at the sign for the Ancient Bristlecone Pine Forest (White Mountain Road) and drive 10 miles to the visitor center parking lot for the Schulman Grove in the White Mountains.

On the trail: This is not the typical rave-worthy hike, but the breathtaking views of the Sierra Crest across the Owens Valley on this off-the-beaten-path jaunt add to the uniqueness of the experience. What makes the hike special is that you and your dog can walk among the oldest living things on earth.

Ancient bristlecone pines have a haunting look.

There are two loop trails to choose from: The barely 1-mile Bristlecone Pine Forest Discovery Trail starts to the left of the visitor center and the two picnic tables. The 4.5-mile Methuselah Trail starts between the visitor center and the picnic tables. The Methuselah Trail protects the oldest of the bristlecone pines (more than 4000 years old), which is not identified. I suspect if it were, some ding-dong would mutilate it with initials or worse, try to take some or all of it home as a trophy.

If the drive and the vista points have eaten away some of your hiking time, I recommend the shorter Discovery Trail. Interpretive signs inform you of the history of the bristlecone pines, which have been designated natural historical monuments. Admire these beautiful specimens along an exposed and scenic stretch of trail with railroad tie steps and several

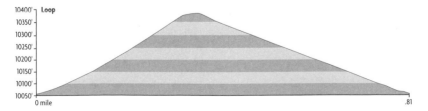

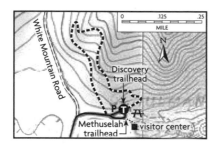

benches. There are no streams or lakes in which your dog can gavotte, but think of the respect he'll get from his canine entourage back home when he barks about the 4000-year-old scents.

If you have time (a slow, two-hour round-trip from Schulman Grove), the inclination, and the appropriate vehicle with a full tank of gas and sufficient water for pooch, consider driving the extra 12 miles that twist, sometimes over rough gravel, along the National Forest Scenic Byway to the Patriarch Grove, home to the largest of these ancient bristlecones. Check with the ranger at the visitor center about road conditions. From the Schulman Visitor Center, turn right and follow the signs along the main gravel road until you come to the turnoff for the byway on your right. Drive 1 mile on a gravel spur road to the parking area. The largest bristlecone pine is actually identified with a plaque along a 0.25-mile interpretive trail that also welcomes dogs on leash. If the natural history doesn't thrill Fido, maybe canine Hollywood trivia will. The fact that Lassie filmed on location in the Patriarch Grove in 1931 might perk up his ears.

INDEPENDENCE

48. Kearsarge Pass

Round-trip: 8.39 miles, OB, or overnight at Gilbert Lake
Hiking time: 4.5–5.5 hours
Elevation range: 9189–11,760 feet
Difficulty: Moderate to strenuous
Season: Summer, fall
Pleasers and teasers: Off leash, lake, no fleas, good overnight; exposed slopes get hot in afternoon sun
Maps: USGS Kearsarge Peak, USGS Mount Clarence King
Information: Inyo National Forest, Mount Whitney Ranger District, (760) 876-6200; Eastern Sierra Interagency Visitor Center (760) 876-6222; *www.fs.fed.us/r5/inyo*

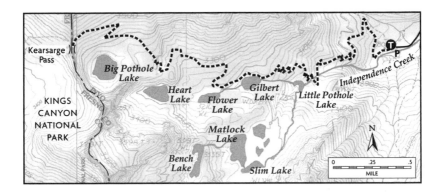

Getting there: From downtown Bishop, drive 41 miles south along Highway 395 to Independence. Turn right on Onion Valley Road and drive 13 miles to the trailhead parking lot at the end of the road.

On the trail: The drive up Onion Valley Road is a prelude to the dramatic scenery that awaits you on the hike. The 4 miles of switchbacks along Independence Creek take you past three lakes and overlooks two more on the way to summiting 11,760-foot Kearsarge Pass, which teeters on the boundary between Inyo National Forest and Kings Canyon National Park.

The trailhead is to the right at the end of the parking lot, where the switchbacks begin to climb right out of the starting gate. At the trail sign for Golden Trout Lake and Kearsarge Pass, stay on the Kearsarge Pass Trail. About 1.5 miles into the hike, the trail skirts Little Pothole Lake on your left and continues switchbacking until the trail narrows into an alley traversing a boulder field just before reaching Gilbert Lake on the left. Gilbert Lake is a superb destination if you don't want to crank to the pass or if you prefer doing an overnight on the trail and saving the pass for a shorter jaunt the next day.

Be sure to encourage your dog to cool off in the water—creek or lake—whenever it's near as the last 2 miles to the pass are exposed and

above tree line, which can also be very hot as well as dry during the summer months. Of course, if you have a lab or a retriever, you'll be more concerned with restraining him from making a beeline for any body of water within a 2-mile radius of the trail.

The last lake along the trail—and a convenient opportunity for pooch to get wet—is Flower Lake. Farther up the trail you'll catch a glimpse of two more lakes—Heart Lake and Big Pothole Lake—tucked in at the base of the glacial slopes on your left. You reach the pass marked by a sign that delineates the border between Inyo National Forest and Kings Canyon National Park, which stretches to the west and is laced with lakes. The beauty along this hike and beyond is as dizzying as the altitude. Enjoy your mountaintop views as you and pooch refuel on snacks and water before retracing your steps to the parking lot. If you have time, enjoy lingering around Gilbert Lake on your way down.

Kearsage Pass, looking west into Kings Canyon. Dogs are not allowed past this point.

Off-trail Perks

The historic Winnedumah Hotel on Highway 395 in downtown Independence is a blast from the past in the most charming way. Clean, well-behaved, housebroken dogs and their responsible owners are welcome to stay in one of the ground-floor guest rooms on three conditions: no dogs on the bed; no dogs left unattended in the room or on the property; dogs must be leashed when walking through the public rooms and around the property.

LONE PINE

49. Lone Pine Lake

Round-trip: 5.54 miles, OB
Hiking time: 3.5–4 hours
Elevation range: 8304–10,077 feet
Difficulty: Moderate
Season: Summer, fall
Pleasers and teasers: Off leash, lake, shade, no fleas, views; pack out your poop area, trail is crowded in summer
Maps: USGS Mount Langley, USGS Mount Whitney
Information: Inyo National Forest, Mount Whitney Ranger District, (760) 876-6200; Eastern Sierra Interagency Visitor Center, (760) 876-6222; *www.fs.fed.us/r5/inyo*

Getting there: From Highway 395 South in the town of Lone Pine, turn right onto Whitney Portal Road, and drive 13 dramatic miles through the Alabama Hills and up to the mountain kingdom of Whitney Portal Recreation Area and the Mount Whitney Trail. The trailhead parking, overflow lots, and picnic areas are at the end of the road.

On the trail: The hike to Lone Pine Lake, set in a natural cathedral of granite spires and peaks, is not only superlatively scenic but also an opportunity to hike along the historic, famous, and heavily traveled Mount Whitney Trail as it climbs 11 miles to the top of the highest peak in the Lower 48. Dogs are welcome on the first 2.8 miles to Lone Pine Lake

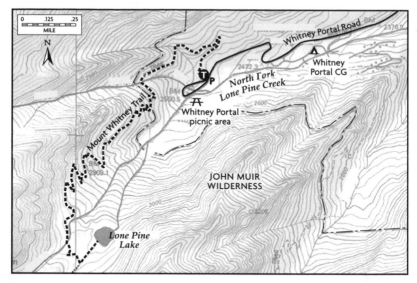

before the trail transitions from Inyo National Forest to Kings Canyon National Park, where dogs are not allowed on trails.

The trailhead is to the right and across the road from the bathrooms and the parking lot. Speaking of bathrooms, hikers are required to pack out dog and human solid waste in the Lone Pine Drainage Area. Call the Mount Whitney Ranger District to find out where to pick up the free waste bags before heading out on the trail or pack your own.

The grade of the trail combined with the altitude makes the switchbacks seem endless, but it's well worth the effort for both you and pooch. The sheer vertical walls of the canyon can make you feel insignificant and minuscule as you climb higher and deeper into the granite fortress shadowed by majestic Mount Whitney.

Halfway to Lone Pine Lake, the North Fork Lone Pine Creek crosses your path as you rock hop across this small but unusually lush oasis bordered by a profusion of ferns.

Just past the creek, you enter the John Muir Wilderness and the scenery returns to High Sierra snapshots of water gliding down the face of tapering ravines below massive rock outcroppings. The last stretch of trail is shaded by stands of pine as you come upon a dozen logs creating a dry footbridge for you and a playful agility course for pooch.

When the trail divides, veer left to Lone Pine Lake, which sits to the left and in a dip below the trail. The lakeshore seems overly trampled, evidence of its popularity, but the lake, shouldered by large boulders and a ring of pines at the far end, seems to hang in the blue sky almost like a landscaped infinity pool. You may not get solitude at Lone Pine Lake, but your pooch will love this high-country playground.

Retrace your steps from the lake and turn right onto the main trail to begin the welcome downhill trek back to the parking lot.

Glasslike surface of Lone Pine Lake

50. Fossil Falls

Round-trip: 0.43 mile, OB
Hiking time: 30 minutes
Elevation range: 3303–3320 feet
Difficulty: Easy, less fit okay
Season: Year-round; in the summer start at sunrise to avoid the heat
Pleasers and teasers: Off leash, unique geology; very hot and dry in summer
Map: USGS Little Lakes
Information: Bureau of Land Management, Ridgecrest Resource Area, (760) 384-5400, *www.ca.blm.gov/ridgecrest*

Getting there: From downtown Lone Pine, drive 45 miles south on Highway 395 and turn left on the aptly named Cinder Road. Drive 0.5 mile to the Bureau of Land Management sign. Bear right and drive 0.5 mile to the parking lot where you'll find an interpretive board, a bathroom, picnic tables, and a campground.

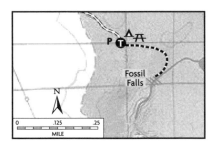

On the trail: This short, unique, and educational hike takes you and pooch across a lava field to a dry lava canyon sculpted by the Owens River 12,000 years ago.

Follow the trail to the rim of the dry falls where both of you can enjoy a scamper atop the smooth, black boulders before retracing your steps back to the parking lot.

Opposite: Now a dry riverbed, Fossil Falls was created when ancient lava flows encountered the Owens River.

KERN PLATEAU AND WESTERN DIVIDE

This section of the Sierra Nevada straddles both the eastern and western slopes, offering stunning views into some of the more remote wilderness areas. You won't find glacial lakes beneath snowcapped peaks, but the vegetative transition from high desert to giant sequoias is quite unique.

SHERMAN PASS

51. Bald Mountain

Round-trip: 0.62 mile, OB
Hiking time: 30 minutes to 1 hour
Elevation range: 9205–9372 feet
Difficulty: Easy, less fit okay
Season: Late spring, summer, fall
Pleasers and teasers: Off leash, shade, views; remote, hot and dry summers
Map: USGS Crag Peak
Information: Sequoia National Forest, Kern River Ranger District, (760) 379-5646, *www.fs.fed.us/r5/sequoia*

Getting there: The long drive to the Bald Mountain Lookout on the Kern Plateau is an unexpected journey of discovery. From Lone Pine, drive

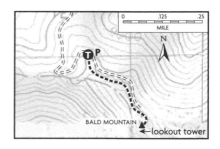

55 miles south on Highway 395 to the Kennedy Meadows turnoff at Nine Mile Canyon Road. Make a right on Nine Mile Canyon Road, and you'll see the BLM sign for Chimney Peak Recreation Area. Nine Mile Road becomes Kennedy Meadows Road at mile 10 where the scenery morphs from roadrunner and yucca desert flatlands to a piñon pine meadow with granite-bulging mountains. Kennedy Meadows Road straightens and levels off as it skirts the South Sierra Wilderness on the right of the meadows and the Domeland Wilderness on the left. You get your first and only peek of Domeland from the road at mile 23. Part of the route shows the devastation of the forest fires that swept across the Domeland Wilderness in 2000–2001 as a result of human carelessness.

Make a left onto Beach Meadows Road around mile 24 where the Kennedy Meadows General Store sits on the right. If you miss the turn and dead-end into Kennedy Meadows Campground, just backtrack to the intersection. Soon after the general store, you will see a sign on the right side of the road for the Kern River South Fork and Sherman Pass Road. If pooch needs a romp and a leg stretch, there's a parking area on the left and a trailhead just past the bridge. Pull over and enjoy a saunter on the trail along this mellow stretch of the Kern River.

Back in the car, continue on Sherman Pass Road. You've traveled about 37 miles from Highway 395. Turn left on Sherman Pass Road at the sign for Sherman Pass, Kernville, Beach Meadows, and Johnsondale. Drive 5 miles to the Bald Mountain Fire Lookout on the left side of Sherman Pass Road. Turn left and drive 2 miles on the dirt road to the parking area just below the lookout. Expect a few rough spots along this road.

In the summer, after your hike you have the option of driving back to

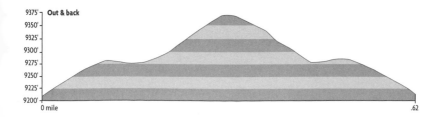

Sacha rests at the fire tower atop Bald Mountain.

Highway 395 or continuing along Sherman Pass Road toward Kernville and other communities on the west side, which are gateways to Highway 101.

On the trail: This easy hike to an operating fire lookout is a real treat. Follow the trail that parallels the road just beyond the locked gate to the base of the lookout. On a clear day, the lookout captures the views over the Domeland and South Sierra Wilderness areas and toward Mineral King and the distant peak of Mount Whitney.

Bald Mountain, in Sequoia National Forest, is one of several fire lookouts on the National Historic Lookout Register. If the forest service or BLM ranger is on duty at the lookout tower, you can climb to the top for a tour, a thrill, and a short shopping spree. Sales from tee shirts go to support the National Historic Lookout Registry, which works to preserve the lookouts.

You'll see a bounty of Sequoia National Forest trailhead signs off Sherman Pass Road for you and pooch to sample the Kern Plateau and break up the drive to and from the fire lookout.

Fire tower atop Bald Mountain

KERNVILLE

52. Dome Rock

Round-trip: 0.35 mile, OB
Hiking time: 30 minutes
Elevation range: 7145–7222 feet
Difficulty: Easy, less fit okay
Seasons: Spring, summer, fall
Pleasers and teasers: Off leash, views; mosquitoes in summer, hot and dry summers
Map: USGS Sentinel Peak
Information: Sequoia National Forest, Tule River–Hot Springs Ranger District, (559) 539-2607, *www.fs.fed.us/r5/sequoia*

Getting there: From Kernville, drive 27 miles north along Sierra Way, past Johnsondale. Bear left where Sierra Way becomes Highway 50 and drive 6 miles to Western Divide Highway. Turn right and drive 12 miles on Western Divide Highway to Dome Rock. Turn right and drive 0.5 mile on

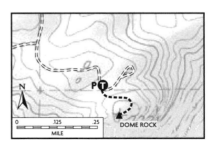

the dirt road bearing left at the fork to the parking area. The trail is left of the bathroom at the locked gate meant to keep vehicles off the Dome.

On the trail: Scamper up the dirt track contouring the mound until you reach the top of the sprawling, smooth granite cap. It's just a skip

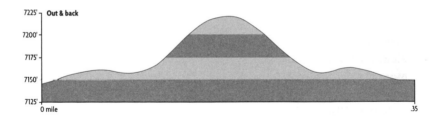

View from Dome Rock across Peppermint Meadows to Sequoia National Forest

and a hop for 360-degree views of the vast wilderness realm that floods the horizon, including the unmistakable Needles and the faint outline of the fire lookout tower perched on a point. While you linger in your daydreams, pooch will be busy darting around with his nose to the granite stone.

53. Trail of 100 Giants

Round-trip: 1.39 miles, L
Hiking time: 1 hour
Elevation range: 6147–6260 feet
Difficulty: Easy, less fit okay
Season: Spring, summer, fall
Pleasers and teasers: Off leash, shade, views; hot summers
Map: USGS Johnsondale
Information: Fee; Sequoia National Forest, Tule River–Hot Springs Ranger District, (559) 539-2607, *www.fs.fed.us/r5/sequoia*

Getting there: From Kernville, drive 27 miles north along Sierra Way past Johnsondale. Bear left where Sierra Way becomes Highway 50 and drive 6 miles to Western Divide Highway. Turn right, drive 2 miles on Western Divide Highway, and turn right into the day-use fee parking lot across the

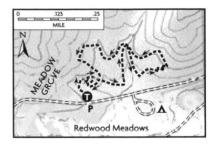

road from the Trail of 100 Giants, just before Redwood Meadows campground. Parking is not allowed on the shoulders of the highway.

On the trail: This is not your classic backcountry hike. But anytime that a trail in the public domain has the appellation national, state, monument, park, or wilderness attached to it in any combination, and it allows dogs, it's a definite go. Those particular labels are usually code for "outstanding natural attributes."

The Trail of 100 Giants—besides offering a rare and remarkably accessible opportunity to admire magnificent specimens of giant sequoia trees, while revering Mother Nature's flawless and astounding creations—has the distinction of being in the Giant Sequoia National Monument. "Monument" is frequently as exclusionary a club as national and state "parks" when it comes to their dog policies.

Put pooch on leash to cross the road and enter the Trail of 100 Giants and begin the loop hike along a paved path past some incredible specimens of giant sequoias. The first tree will blow your mind and would take your dog most of day to sniff all the way around it. Follow this impressively appointed interpretive trail with its many benches and footbridges as it meanders, rolls, and loops past several unique examples of giant sequoias clustered in this protected glen.

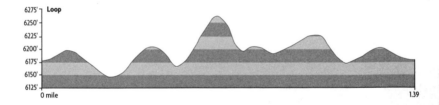

Opposite: A trio of giant sequoias

54. North Fork Kern River Trail

Round-trip: 1.58 miles, OB
Hiking time: 1–1.5 hours
Elevation range: 3782–3896 feet
Difficulty: Easy, less fit okay
Seasons: Spring, summer, fall
Pleasers and teasers: Off leash, river; hot summers, litter in primitive riverside campsites
Map: USGS Fairview
Information: Sequoia National Forest, Kern River Ranger District, Lake Isabella Visitor Center, (760) 379-5646, *www.fs.fed.us/r5/sequoia*

Getting there: From Kernville, drive 22 miles north along Sierra Way to the Johnsondale bridge across the Kern River, just before entering Giant Sequoia National Monument. There's a larger parking lot on the north side of the bridge to the right of the road where white-water rafters put in.

On the trail: Anything as rare as Wild and Scenic that can be accessed on foot is worth checking out. Walk back across the hikers bridge and go down the metal stairway to the trail and river. The trail officially follows the Wild and Scenic North Fork upstream for 5.2 miles along a well-worn but narrow, rugged path on the slope above the river. Unfortunately, the occasional primitive fishermen spur trails that lead to the water's edge have been shamefully spoiled by fire rings full of litter.

That being said, let's focus on the positive and the fact that there's something precious about any place with a river running through it. Kern River canyon is impressive at every bend. In the late season or following

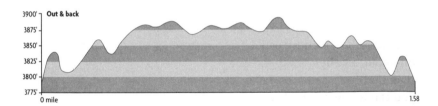

Stepping around beaver tail cactus near the trail

a low precipitation winter when the water level has dropped and the flow has mellowed, the exposed stretch of beach closest to the stairway is a pleasant launching pad for water-loving dogs, following a leisurely one-hour hike up the canyon and back, to get the flavor of the untamed river that owns the scenic Kern canyon. If time and conditions permit, you can follow the trail farther up the canyon.

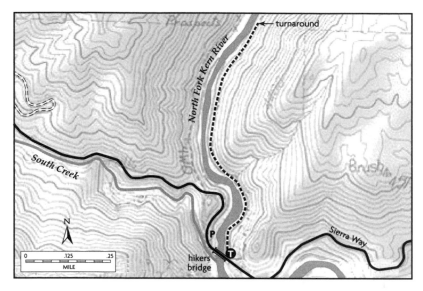

Be aware that even late in the season, the current can be swift in the center of the river, so be wise. If your dog is a paddler rather than a hardy swimmer or a crazed retriever of buoyant toys, let him have fun with the security of an extendable leash clipped to his harness for two reasons: If dogs were meant to float down rapids, they would quack. A tired dog can turn into a drowned dog.

55. Sunday Peak

Round-trip: 3.42 miles, OB
Hiking time: 2.5 hours
Elevation range: 7219–8295 feet
Difficulty: Moderate
Season: Spring, summer, fall
Pleasers and teasers: Off leash, shade, views; mosquitoes in summer, summer afternoons can be hot
Map: USGS Tobias Peak
Information: Sequoia National Forest, Kernville Ranger District, Lake Isabella Visitor Center, (760) 379-5646, *www.fs.fed.us/r5/sequoia*

Getting there: From Kernville drive 4.3 miles south to Wofford Heights on the west shore of Lake Isabella. Turn right onto Highway 155 West

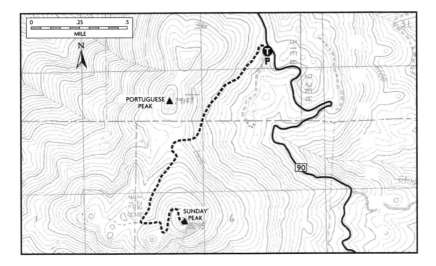

and drive 7.5 miles to Greenhorn Summit. Make a right at the Greenhorn Summit sand shed across from Rancheria Road and just past the sign for Shirley Meadows and Rancheria Road. Follow the road just right of the sand shed, and you'll see a sign on the right for Portuguese Pass Road 24S15/Forest Road 90. Follow the forest service road 6.5 miles to the Sunday Peak parking area on the left. The trail begins just above and to the right of the parking area.

On the trail: The dry, shaded hike beneath the canopy of conifers along loose dirt and pine mulch accented by decorator boulders is easy on the paws, and the wide-angle perspective from the top, a visual treat. The hike kicks off with a stiff ascent before tapering off to a more gradual incline. A trail marker along the way indicates that you are hiking in the Giant Sequoia National Monument.

The trail bends northeast past a clearing of fallen and snapped trees as the landscape transitions from forest to scrub. Around the mound, it leads

Signing the trail log atop Sunday Peak

you to the stack of granite slabs that rise as Sunday Peak. The views unfurl now over the hazy lowlands west and a staggered stadium of ranges and peaks north, south, and east beyond the Kern valley. A small, weathered wooden box secured by a rock sits like a time capsule, waiting for hikers to record their presence. Like the ritual signing of a guest book, most visitors write a comment alongside their name, date, and hometown. While some leave their mountaintop inspirations on paper, others leave small personal paraphernalia like playing cards and topo maps, almost as a nostalgic offering to the gods and ghosts of vanishing fire towers and their keepers, guardians of our wilderness.

Alex wanted to leave his favorite toy from this hike. Thankfully, the well-chewed and goobered limb was twice the size of the box, and I was able to dissuade him from trying to fit it in the box.

Retrace your steps and let your dog show you how to enjoy a carefree gallivant down the gradual slope to the parking lot.

APPENDIX

Recommended Reading

Acker, Randy. *Field Guide to Dog First Aid: Emergency Care of the Outdoor Dog*. Belgrade, MT: Wilderness Adventure Press, 1999.

Berger, Karen. *Backpacking and Hiking*. New York: DK Eyewitness Guides, 2005.

Burns, Mike, and Bob Burns. *Wilderness Navigation*. Seattle: The Mountaineers Books, 2004.

Faculty of the Cummings School of Veterinary Medicine at Tufts University. Edited by Nicholas Dodman, BVMS. *Puppy's First Steps: The Whole Dog Approach*. New York: Houghton Mifflin Company, 2007.

Mehus-Roe, Kristin. *The Original Dog Bible: The Definitive Source to All Things Dog*. Irvine, CA: Bowtie Press, 2005.

Mullally, Linda. *Hiking with Dogs: Becoming a Wilderness Wise Dog Owner*. Guildford, CT: Falcon Guides, 2006.

Reisner, Mark. *Cadillac Desert*. New York: Penguin Books, 1993.

Sierra Club. *San Luis Obispo County Trail Guide*. Santa Lucia Chapter, 1981.

Online Dog Gear and Supplies

www.drfostersmith.com
www.expeditionoutfittersonline.com
www.our-pets.com
www.rei.com
www.ruffwear.com
www.wolfpacks.com

Outdoor Recreation Resources and Useful Contacts

American Automobile Association, dog-friendly lodging and campground info: *www.AAA.com*

Articles, studies, and health alerts: *www.workingdogs.com*

Bureau of Land Management: *www.blm.gov/*

Giant Sequoia National Monument: *www.fs.fed.us/r5/sequoia/*

National Forest maps: *www.fs.fed.us/maps/*

Nonprofit lobbying group for dog owners on public land:
www.caldog.org

Topographical maps: *www.maps.nationalgeographic.com/topo/*

Nature Conservation/Historical Preservation and Hiker Education

American Hiking Society: *www.americanhiking.org*

Big Sur Land Trust: *www.bigsurlandtrust.org*

California State Parks Foundation: *www.calparks.org*

Leave No Trace for Outdoor Ethics and Skills: *www.lnt.org*

National Historic Lookout Register: *www.firetower.org*

National Parks Conservation Association: *www.npca.org*

National Resource Defense Council: *www.nrdc.org*

National Wildlife Federation: *www.nwf.org*

Nature Conservancy: *www.nature.org*

Sierra Club: *www.sierraclub.org*

The Wilderness Society: *www.wilderness.org*

Emergency Numbers for Your First-Aid Kit

American Veterinary Association, (800) 248-2862

National Animal Poison Control Center (ASPCA), (888) 426-4435

Animal Advocacy and Education

People for the Ethical Treatment of Animals: *www.peta.org*

The United States Humane Society: *www.hsus.org/pets*

INDEX

ABOUT THE AUTHORS

*D*avid Mullally, a native Californian, and Quebec-born Linda Mullally have been a husband and wife team on life's adventure for twenty-four years. He, an attorney, and she, a sports massage therapist, express their creative spirits and passion for world travel and nature through writing and photography for magazines and newspapers. When in California, David and Linda divide their time between the Monterey Peninsula on the Central Coast and Mammoth Lakes in the Eastern Sierra.

The sixteen years spent exploring hiking trails and dog-friendly hangouts across the United States and Canada for Fancy Publications with their two coyote-husky companions, Lobo and Shiloh, remain among their most cherished adventure travel memories. For the last two years they have filled the void of Lobo and Shiloh's passing with teaching the joys of the trail to friends' dogs, Murphy, Alex, and Moses.

Linda continues to share her experiences and educates the public on responsible dog ownership. *Best Hikes with Dogs: Central California* is David and Linda's third book, with several titles in progress.

THE MOUNTAINEERS, founded in 1906, is a nonprofit outdoor activity and conservation club, whose mission is "to explore, study, preserve, and enjoy the natural beauty of the outdoors...." Based in Seattle, Washington, the club is now the third-largest such organization in the United States, with seven branches throughout Washington State.

The Mountaineers sponsors both classes and year-round outdoor activities in the Pacific Northwest, which include hiking, mountain climbing, ski-touring, snowshoeing, bicycling, camping, kayaking, nature study, sailing, and adventure travel. The club's conservation division supports environmental causes through educational activities, sponsoring legislation, and presenting informational programs.

All club activities are led by skilled, experienced instructors, who are dedicated to promoting safe and responsible enjoyment and preservation of the outdoors.

If you would like to participate in these organized outdoor activities or the club's programs, consider a membership in The Mountaineers. For information and an application, write or call The Mountaineers, Club Headquarters, 300 Third Avenue West, Seattle, WA 98119; 206-284-6310. You can also visit the club's website at www.mountaineers.org or contact The Mountaineers via email at *clubmail@mountaineers.org*.

The Mountaineers Books, an active, nonprofit publishing program of the club, produces guidebooks, instructional texts, historical works, natural history guides, and works on environmental conservation. All books produced by The Mountaineers Books fulfill the club's mission.

Send or call for our catalog of more than 500 outdoor titles:

The Mountaineers Books
1001 SW Klickitat Way, Suite 201
Seattle, WA 98134
800-553-4453
mbooks@mountaineersbooks.org
www.mountaineersbooks.org

The Mountaineers Books is proud to be a corporate sponsor of The Leave No Trace Center for Outdoor Ethics, whose mission is to promote and inspire responsible outdoor recreation through education, research, and partnerships. The Leave No Trace program is focused specifically on human-powered (nonmotorized) recreation.

Leave No Trace strives to educate visitors about the nature of their recreational impacts, as well as offer techniques to prevent and minimize such impacts. Leave No Trace is best understood as an educational and ethical program, not as a set of rules and regulations.

For more information, visit *www.LNT.org,* or call 800-332-4100.

OTHER TITLES YOU MIGHT ENJOY FROM THE MOUNTAINEERS BOOKS

BEST HIKES WITH DOGS:
Southern California
Allen Riedel
Take your four-legged
friend on an adventure.

UNLEASHED:
Climbing Canines, Hiking
Hounds, Fishing Fidos,
and other Daring Dogs
Lisa Wogan
Action-loving dogs!

WATERFALL LOVER'S GUIDE
TO NORTHERN CALIFORNIA
Matt & Krissi Danielsson
Visit more than 300 waterfalls
in Northern California.

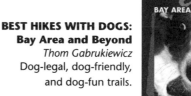

BEST HIKES WITH DOGS:
Bay Area and Beyond
Thom Gabrukiewicz
Dog-legal, dog-friendly,
and dog-fun trails.

OUTDOORS ONLINE
Erika Dillman
The only honest
evaluation of all things
outdoorsy on the web.

DON'T FORGET
THE DUCT TAPE
Kristin Hostetter
Secrets to saving
your trip from disaster.

Find The Mountaineers Books' entire catalog of
outdoor titles online at *www.mountaineersbooks.org*.